"At a time when our cultural lack of understanding of the birth process has reached an extreme degree, the world needs practitioners such as Mia Kalef."

> —**Michel Odent, MD, author of** *Childbirth and the Future of Homo Sapiens*

"Mia Kalef provides major evidence for the existence of sentience and experience in the womb. She defends with good arguments that our collective denial of this truth impacts negatively how we deal with pregnancy and prenatal mother-child interaction, which itself leads to severe disturbances in our relationships with ourselves, each other, and the global community of life. She provides clear and efficient procedures to help us recognize and overcome early traumatic imprints so that we may be in harmony with the stream of life. This book is a firm and reliable plea to reevaluate the secret life of babies and see how they are emissaries of a lost wisdom that has the power to set us on a more wholesome and balanced course."

> —**Jaap Van Der Wal, PhD, author of** *The Embryo in Us,* **and former professor of anatomy and embryology, University of Maastricht, Holland**

"Mia Kalef has written a book that brings science to a level from which everyone can understand and benefit. She cites interesting studies from around the world ... animals, the human species, history, and various cultures. With vivid and yet simple depictions of how prenatal and birth experiences can support a person's/family's quest for change and health, her words remind us that it is never too late to heal."

> —**Judyth O. Weaver, PhD, somatic and perinatal therapist, and co-founder and professor, Santa Barbara Graduate Institute**

"It's a pleasure to read Dr. Kalef's comprehensive and empathetic book, in which she describes the deep influences human early life have on later physical, emotional, and social conditions. She describes the social and historical backgrounds for why we don't know this and invites us to her Intuitive Recovery Project for finding a new, more sustainable personal connection to these concepts. This great book helps us understand the very real social implications of the prenatal time and to deepen our understanding of ourselves within it."

—Rupert Linder, MD, past president, International Society of Prenatal and Perinatal Psychology and Medicine, and specialist for gynecology, obstetrics, psychosomatics, and psychotherapy

"Dr. Mia Kalef's *The Secret Life of Babies* is an illuminating read, and a revelation. Not only a book for new and expecting parents, Kalef's book will make readers think about the circumstances surrounding their own birth and how this could be the basis of some of the traumas and inhibitions, and even addictions they experience as adults. Incorporating both detailed case studies and broader overviews of history and culture, the book is a wake-up call for people to pay more attention to prenatal and perinatal conditions and take a hard look at the way that society treats women and mothers, and ask themselves if it's time for a change."

—Jenny Uechi, managing editor, *The Vancouver Observer*

The Secret Life
of Babies

How Our Prebirth and Birth
Experiences Shape Our World

MIA KALEF, DC

Foreword by Andrew Feldmar

North Atlantic Books
Berkeley, California

Published by
North Atlantic Books
P.O. Box 12327
Berkeley, California 94712

Cover and book design by Suzanne Albertson
Cover image © Sergey Nivens/Shutterstock.com

Printed in the United States of America

William Stafford, excerpt from "Climbing Along the River" from *The Way It Is: New and Selected Poems*. Copyright © 1991, 1998 by William Stafford and the Estate of William Stafford. Reprinted with the permission of The Permissions Company, Inc. on behalf of Graywolf Press, Minneapolis, Minnesota, www.graywolfpress.org.

The Secret Life of Babies: How Our Prebirth and Birth Experiences Shape Our World is sponsored by the Society for the Study of Native Arts and Sciences, a nonprofit educational corporation whose goals are to develop an educational and cross-cultural perspective linking various scientific, social, and artistic fields; to nurture a holistic view of arts, sciences, humanities, and healing; and to publish and distribute literature on the relationship of mind, body, and nature.

North Atlantic Books' publications are available through most bookstores. For further information, visit our website at www.northatlanticbooks.com or call 800-733-3000.

Library of Congress Cataloging-in-Publication Data

Kalef, Mia, 1972–
    The secret life of babies: how our prebirth and birth experiences shape our world
    / Mia Kalef; foreword by Andrew Feldmar.
        pages cm
    Includes bibliographical references and index.
    ISBN 978-1-58394-803-3 (pbk.: alk. paper)
1. Infant psychology. 2. Infant development. I. Title.
    BF719.K35 2014
    155.42'2—dc23
    2013026870

1 2 3 4 5 6 7 8 9 SHERIDAN 18 17 16 15 14

Printed on recycled paper

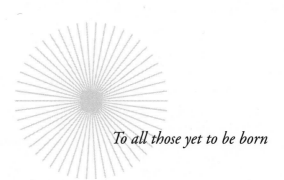

To all those yet to be born

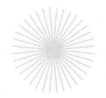

The Embryo is the Universe writing itself on its own Body.

—Richard Grossinger, *Embryogenesis: Species, Gender,*
and Identity

CONTENTS

PART THREE: Marriage

CHAPTER 5

CHAPTER 6

FOREWORD

Although without exception, in all cultures, past and present, all human beings share very similar beginnings; by the time we are adults, we can hardly recollect this source of shared humanity. All newborns are Stone-Age babies but born now to twenty-first century mothers of vastly different cultures, nations, and circumstances.

How this entry is negotiated; how sensitively we welcome and adapt *to* the new arrival; and how forcefully, impatiently, and ignorantly we demand adaptation *from* the baby—these all shape and determine later habit patterns, hopes and fears, character, personality, and the unique flavor of being oneself in the world.

There is no organism without an environment. As soon as my father's sperm spilled its genetic load into my mother's egg, the very moment the zygote that was my beginning clicked into being, I was already in my mother's fallopian tube. The environment/organism interaction can be +, −, or 0. The environment can be facilitating, nourishing, supportive, hostile, destructive, exploiting, or neutral (neither + nor −). Evidence from various sources indicates that we remember these interactions and, at a perhaps cellular level, learn to anticipate more of what our experience was. We project into the future what has already happened. A run of + sets us up for expecting more +, a run of −, similarly. This might explain the tragic truth that the rich get richer and the poor get poorer.

Otto Rank, Nandor Fodor, Francis J. Mott, Lietaert Peerbolte, Frank Lake, R. D. Laing, Stanislav Grof, Elizabeth Fehr, and Thomas R. Verny—just to mention a few—by now have explored, pioneered, and mapped out the birth realm against overwhelming skepticism, opposition, and ridicule. Mia Kalef's book belongs in this tradition.

Read her carefully. I believe, with Michele Odent, that loving, careful attention to the early days of a creature can make later life easier, more joyous, more fulfilling, less crazed, gentler, and more loving. What could be more urgent, more important?

Andrew Feldmar

PREFACE

Since writing the first drafts of *The Secret Life of Babies,* several years' worth of feedback, teaching, public speaking, private practice, and deep living—as well as countless hours of contemplation—have deepened, humbled, and transformed this work and me. My revisions have caused me to acknowledge two inherent challenges of committing a nonfiction book to print.

First, inherently, a book can only act as a snapshot capturing the whole of the writer's intentions intended to then go on and serve as an accurate and enduring precipitate of his or her worldview even *after the time of writing.* I have come to accept that the contents—of this book, at least—may appear unchanging, even as my lens and the lens of the world sharpens, defines, and evolves. Therefore, despite the temptation to reach a final conclusion regarding what this book is or I am about, I ask you to consider this book (and every book) a feature within my, and maybe your, living river—one of the moving pieces continually coming downstream toward or past you, reflecting differently depending on the light and season, or on how long any of us swim or paddle alongside it. My wish is that, from wherever you watch, you encounter your own perspective, color, and experience.

The second challenge is well stated by Stephen Jenkinson, one of my teachers, who has said, "To write anything down is to forget it." Although every oral tradition that's still intact knows this, I have nonetheless accepted that my way of passing this story along is to write it down. I have attempted to "remarry" the written to the oral, which is why I have styled this book as a conversation designed to humbly approach the ancient practice of storytelling.

There are a few other points about the writing that I would like to speak to.

I sometimes refer to babies as "she" or "he." This does not denote a gender preference but is done to simplify what would otherwise appear awkwardly as "he or she" repeatedly through the book.

Everything I speak of in this book I have experienced firsthand, either in my clinical practice or as a participant in my own therapy. Many of the journals and studies I cite serve to support content that appears surprising. There are also some studies so compelling that I share them because I believe they have the power to reshape society. All names of patients have been changed and permission sought to share their stories.

This book arose from a lifelong joy in writing and from the knowledge that I want to share this particular message: I am indebted to our consciousness, who, no matter how insufficient a home we have made for over millennia, continues to honor us by courting us back into relationship with its mystifying ways, *even* after years of going underground. These pages are my best way at this time to share my reverence for a particular aspect of consciousness, babies' consciousness—both in and out of the womb—and how early consciousness persists rather than recedes throughout life until death. I anticipate that the contents here are at times hard to read, but I believe that perpetuating the global conversation about early human consciousness is an essential ingredient to sustainability.

Although I've just given away the thesis of this book, it doesn't matter. The thesis is worth repeating, and I do just that again and again, in different ways. I find that, no matter where I turn, I see evidence of our early sentience and reasons individuals and societies have lost their reverence for the unseen living us. I share with you what I see. We look at history, sociology, anthropology, medicine, religion, real-life case studies, and more.

I have one last comment: I experience babies as one of the world's *wordless teachers*. Others are trees, animals, wind, snow, and rivers, to name a few. It is my intention here to weave a logically sound, creatively joyous, heartbreakingly sobering treatise on how babies are one of the unacknowledged emissaries, seers, and key interpreters of what seems largely mysterious about many of the planet's present-day challenges. I use these adjectives consciously and carefully because they describe the experience I have in my work and what I think about when I'm writing to you.

When I attune myself so that I am truly "with a baby," I receive a gift that, for me, is akin to prayer, ceremony, revelation, grace, and redemption. It is intoxicating and humbling, and even though I have done my best to write it all down, I have learned that things, big things, are at times beyond modern words' capacity to hold.

Having said that, reclaiming my relationship with the sentience of early life seems like one of the most direct ways for my humanity to come home and, once home, to stay home. I am grateful to share what matters most to me with you. Thank you for reading.

INTRODUCTION

The Myth
Science and Experience

Most of the seats are still empty, the lights dimmed. Small groups of people speak quietly in pockets around the room. I stand in one corner, watching the stage. In a short time it will be my turn. Breathing in deeply, I remind myself why I have come, and as I search for the message that wants to be told, I close my eyes. A long-forgotten story begins to take shape in my mind's eye:

> Two Great Lovers, Science and Experience, lived harmoniously together. All they have touched has become whole, as their union provided trust for those who yearned to find it. Their wholeness, being complete, contained within it all knowledge. One year, while sailing between shores to those in need, Science and Experience encountered dark skies. As the grey skies turned to rain and the seas lashed angrily, they gathered preciously closer. But the strength of the lovers' unity could not hold their ship, and each was flung ruthlessly into the waters. Science was cast to one shore and Experience to another, while the safely love-locked knowledge between them scattered out onto the sea bottom.
>
> Having never been separated, Science and Experience felt a lack, but having never known separation, they did not recognize their division and continued their work without the other. As best they could, each brought trust to those who yearned to find it. Each learned to get along without the other, and as time passed, they adjusted to being apart until one day they forgot how it used to be.

From that day on, Science, on his shore, collected evidence. He found that evidence helped others believe that it was safe to trust. He worked tirelessly and meticulously and was well loved for his contribution. Yet despite his thorough methods, Science could not find evidence to trust the thoughts he had been having, which suggested that there was something more.

Experience also worked steadfastly on her shore. She collected feelings. She inspired trust by reteaching those who needed to feel. Experience was well loved for her teachings. But despite her subtle skills, Experience was troubled that her teachings could not reach everyone. She longed for help, knowing there was more.

The disbanded lovers, unknowing in their separation, missed the knowledge born only from their union.

One day, while walking by the ocean, Experience saw her reflection in a retreating wave. While she could see her image in the rushing froth, a curious sight caught her attention. Another face emerged behind her reflection. Perplexed, she asked aloud, "Has so much time gone by that I do not recognize myself?" Experience paused and nodded silently as she contemplated the two reflections. Yes, she thought, I have forgotten something. Moons and oceans ago, I knew no separation. Something was whole that I do not have now. She continued to stare into the wave as it receded, the faces with it. Experience stared a while longer, struggling to remember what lingered in the tide. With that, Experience cast a deep intention out into the sea and whispered a wish: "Reveal to me what I have forgotten."

Science, compelled by his ever-growing, unexplainable thoughts of more, strode alone down to his shore. The words of his contemplation were interrupted by a deep, quiet voice, one not unlike his own, rising gently in his ears. It seemed to come from somewhere beyond the wind and from deep under the sea. Science paused and looked around. He could see no other on the shore to explain the sound, so he asked aloud, "Your sound is not my voice, and it is not my language, but I understand every word. Who are you?" He quieted his mind so as not to miss the precious utterings, and he thought he made out a whisper: "We were once together."

And then, just like the storm that had torn the lovers apart years earlier, clouds gathered and the seas swayed. From Experience's shore, the two faces, reflecting deep beneath a wave, drove toward the center of the sea. Experience, despite the growing tempest, waded in to follow them. And on Science's shore, the whispering words swirling in the air spiraled out as well. Science followed the pleasing sounds, letting himself be pulled out into the rising swells. The ocean churned the long-lost lovers with determination, pulling them forward and closer. Neither fought, neither feared. The waters glided around them, tracing their shapes under the darkening skies.

As the waters stilled, a warm light shone through from the bottom of the sea, and up—as if it had never known its loss—rose the long-buried, love-locked Knowledge. Experience, calm but exhausted, opened her eyes. Science, with his ears still set on the voice, swam closer.

Experience looked up from the glow beneath her feet. Before her eyes could adjust, she could sense him. "Yes," she said aloud, reaching out into the water, "we were once together."

Science, now able to hear the voice, knew what the feeling of more had been and nodded, reaching to touch her in the shifting light and dark. "Yes, we were once together." As the threading waters knit slowly around the lovers, the long-lost Knowledge . . .

My eyes open. The people in the room are settling in and are getting ready for me to speak.

The doctors, some still checking their phones, look on impatiently, willingly, and indifferently. The stage is now illuminated. These men and women have come to listen to my lecture on infant awareness and how it relates to obstetrics. Provided for us on the screen is a list of developmental milestones that typical babies go through in the womb and in the months after birth. The doctors study the screen and compare their knowledge to the list. I too consider the information. I look at my audience and take a deep breath.

"It is because of you that knowledge exists."

Although some look doubtful, all eyes shoot up in attention and focus on me.

I continue. "If it weren't for you and all the doctors and scientists in the world who have ever tended to a pregnant mother or newborn baby, science would have nothing to record!"

The attendees start shifting in their seats, some looking at the others.

"Without the courage you've had to bring your attention to the intimate mystery of life unfolding, studying and serving for years, often without sleep or time for anything else, science would have nothing to offer. Century after century, science and medicine have attempted to unravel what nature has always known. The path has not been clear or always simple. You doing what you do, century after century, has given science a story to tell.

"Hundreds of years ago, in the mechanistic age of the seventeenth century, two lovers, destined for unity, were separated. The change in the world was seen in humans too. The population naturally gravitated to one of two groups, made up of those who trusted evidence and science, or those who trusted feelings and instincts. When I see you here, with your deep professional prowess, along with your accolades, and then I think back to the reasons you found your life path to your work—the tender moments in your youth that made you curious, vulnerable, discerning, wanting to help or understand how the body works—I see two disparate lovers looking across the room at each other. Great knowledge emerges in the space between you. Your gifts, which you offer people, represent the embodiment of the knowledge created by both."

I am inspired by the rising attention in the room. I go on with my lecture, and for those moments, centuries of separation seem to give way, and this sprawling dark room witnesses a timeless love. The Great Marriage between Science and Experience rekindles as I sense the audience fill with remembering.

There was a time when all of us were babies. *Their* Knowledge is also *ours.*

The Quest: Sparking the Conversation

Secretly, in small pockets within hospitals, birthing centers, therapists' offices, schools, homes, and communities, a movement is stirring, a remembering of Knowledge. One aspect of this movement, which I call *emergent culture,* includes reexamining how children are brought into this world. They are asking questions about the roots of our cultural habits in the face of some of the most troubling times in the history of human birth and culture as a whole. As cutting-edge scientists, therapists, birth supports, doctors, and parents continue to gather in far too small numbers to discuss the future of our culture, I invite you to consider the power you have to shape a road of peacefulness and contentedness, where all children are supported to live in their authenticity, right from the beginning.

Consider the conversation we're about to have regarding a culture shift, a form of global activism, and of social justice that is also undergoing its own birth process. Imagine the world is urging powerful contractions and that the movement takes humans on a quest to remarry the literal and the mythological Science with Experience. Take up this quest and join the generations that will be remembered for recognizing and celebrating the importance of the time from preconception through the first birthday, and the influence this period has on how people treat themselves, others, and the planet.

The stories, scientific studies, and real-life case studies in this book can help you turn toward babies and even toward the baby you once were. This "turning toward" stands to help sustain the health of humans in relationship to each other and to the world.

My proposal is that when societies once again honor the intelligence and sentience of their babies, even before they are conceived, then they and the incoming next generation by consequence honor all living things in the world. The changes will be seen economically, by the resolution of poverty; ecologically, as children who are raised with compassion will naturally care for the living things around them; and socially, as violence becomes obsolete in the face of cooperation.

As a doctor, a healer, a scientist, a future mother, but mostly as a curious human being, I am compelled to share all this with you. I also invite you to share this book with your family, friends, and colleagues; use the questions it raises to begin a dialogue that will intersect with and advance the great debates of our time and, with them, promote a worldwide transformation.

Who Is This Book For?

Unless you are pregnant or a new parent, you might be unlikely to pick up a book that has "babies" in the title. If you are not at that stage of life when babies are in—or will soon be in—your immediate world, you may have little interest in thinking about them.

There are layers of reasons for this. The first layer might be practical: out of sight, out of mind. In Western culture, where families live separately, adults may go weeks without seeing a baby. In villages and traditional families, where people often live together, every generation is visible in daily life.

The second layer might be the result of societal pressures: An interest in babies exposes a certain vulnerability. Unless a person is at the stage of life when marriage and childbearing is the norm, the tenderness required for babies may not appear masculine or sexy, or it may classify a man as having "too soft a side," or a woman as having a "biological clock ticking down." Most people in Western culture prefer to avoid these forms of ridicule.

The third layer is also social: Unless you are good with babies—able to quiet a crying little one or engage them in curiosity or laughter—they can be embarrassing. Are you quick to pass a baby back to the person you know will comfort her when she suddenly breaks into tears in your arms? Who wants to be seen holding an inconsolable baby?

The fourth layer is economic: In a capitalist or materialist society like today's, babies can slow people down. This type of society risks being less productive, maybe less successful, possibly even less intelligent, if individuals spend time with, or think about, babies, who, after all, don't make money.

A fifth layer is personal: We often consider babies a different species—vulnerable, sensitive, and unable to communicate as adults do. But wait, weren't you a baby once, too? Wasn't everyone? Perhaps you remember all too well how you were once that dependent, vulnerable, available, and sincere. But like most people, you might think those characteristics are best forgotten in today's world.

There are, however, benefits to being dependent, vulnerable, available, and sincere, and those benefits are the big secret in this book's title. In truth, this book is not simply about babies. It's about babies and the adults they become. It's about you and about how your earliest experiences not only shaped your health but also collectively shaped this powerful and delicate world you inhabit. It's about societies as a whole and all their members.

My goal is to remove the secrecy from the life of babies and open the way to their magical world, one you may have already sensed or remember is there. This world has existed, like a promise-in-waiting, as hundreds of years of cultural habits have steered most away from seeing it. The gateway to this magical world is not far from here. As you will see, hidden doorways are everywhere, and when you apply your curiosity, the alchemy that occurs breaks down barriers, giving rise to great freedom to explore. Without your curiosity, the world-in-waiting remains concealed.

When people, no matter their age, create an environment that allows them to enter and decode their secret worlds, they discover a surprising amount of content from the time between their conception and the end of their first year of life, events very few people have conscious memory of. When these revelations are processed, individuals find their body becomes freer, their emotions more available and balanced, and their life easier and more fulfilling. This may sound great, or it may seem daunting. The process is not easy, nor is it for the faint-of-heart, but it is extremely worthwhile. A repair process occurs in which a new depth of love emerges, love for others and for oneself. And although it may sound utopian, this noticeable love seems to extend to the rest of humankind and the planet as well.

If you are present to babies and young children, whether they are a thought in your mind or alive in your belly, home, hands, or schools, you will learn what they want you to know. It will take patience, because children have an ancient, unchanged language, made nearly extinct through centuries of society's habitual deafness. In this book, I attempt to open your senses so you can again—even more than before—hear, feel, see, smell, and taste the sensual world, the sentient world, of which babies, along with animals and nature, are stewards.

This book explores foundational movements of life. It explains the energetic, chemical, and relational influences of brain development and the physiology of attachment, and it introduces you to the *family field,* a paradigm and healing model used to help decode what pre- and postnatal babies can teach about their surroundings. It explains historical and present-day indicators that strongly suggest to critics that we do, in fact, retain memories from these early times—memories that shape health both personally and culturally. *The Secret Life of Babies* includes a simple, easy-to-implement process, the Intuitive Recovery Project (IRP), which helps remove the barriers that have grown over your senses.

The message of this book will, therefore, be valuable for parents, health-care providers, businesspeople, spiritual leaders, policy makers, and even for your relationship with yourself. Included are stories about real people who have recovered forgotten aspects of themselves that they found locked in their secret world. This book will help you learn about yourself by understanding babies. Their unchanged language, with its majestic pace and volume, tempo and timbre, can turn skilled and willing listeners into pivotal witnesses and participants in recovering our world.

A Song Worth Singing

It has been said that there are tribes in East Africa that count the birth date of a child, not from the day she is born or even from the time she is conceived, but from the moment she is simply a thought in her mother's mind. Aware of a father she intends to conceive with, the mother goes to sit under a tree until she can hear the song of her child. She teaches the song to her husband so that they can sing it together while they make love, inviting the child to join them. They then teach it to the midwives and the elders of the village so that they too can sing the song at the child's miraculous moment of birth. The villagers sing the song to the child in times of triumph and trouble. It is sung during the wedding ceremony. And when loved ones gather around the deathbed, they sing the song for the last time.[1] What would our lives be like if we did as indigenous people, who seem to understand sentience begins long before birth, do? What kind of world would we live in if we knew children were present this early?

When I heard this story, it confirmed thousands of hands-on sessions I had done with patients over my years of practice. It is also backed by eighty years of scientific research and the work of my predecessors and mentors, the likes of which are Michel Odent, Ray Castellino, Myrna Martin, Michael Trout, and Andrew Feldmar to name a few—all who say our experiences in the womb and at birth shape our lives. I've become concerned about how we treat babies, both in and out of the womb. It's as though we, in our modern technological societies, don't believe that birth and prebirth have long-term consequences at all. We've made it OK to do things to babies that hurt and scare them. Interventions like induction, epidural, forceps, vacuum, Cesarean, separating babies from birth, and significant procedures during pregnancy all have become matter of course even when not medically necessary. These procedures teach babies that feeling hurt, scared, and medicated are normal expectations of themselves and the world. The cost is huge. The implications are far reaching—some of which don't even show up until later in life—in the form of sleeping challenges, eating challenges, depression, low self-esteem, anxiety, and at worst, violence, addictions, and even suicide. These same consequences have been shown in my patients time and time again. I have even uncovered aspects to my own behaviors by looking at my birth and prebirth.

I'm compelled to share my life experiences, and my work is guided by four key principles. One, babies remember their experiences, which means all the way back to conception. Two, consciousness precedes brain structure, which means we have memories even before we develop our brains. Three, babies are barometers, which means to say that their symptoms are a reflection of the greater environment, which includes their families, our societies, and our ancestries. Four, it's never too late to heal. What I propose in this book is to flesh out these four principles and add a critical review of history, case studies, and scientific evidence to further reveal the heart of the problem. I also intend to make suggestions about how we might deal with the consequences of what's already been done and make suggestions about how we can transform our relationship with babies by addressing how we treat our bodies and nature. It is my intention to inspire awareness and promote change. Perhaps by attuning our listening we may come to hear our songs that have always been there, just waiting to be sung.

PART ONE

Science

CHAPTER 1

The First Principle
Babies Remember Their Experiences

Wholeness does not have a direction from one thing to another. When the master enters the waiting room, the process of nothingness, of not being, of poverty, maturates to the point where all we know is the presence of the indwelling master, the indwelling health that is us. It is not within us and it is not in us—it is in everything.

—James Jealous, *Wholeness No. 1*

The Controversy

What does it mean to remember an experience? Where does memory reside? In the mind? And if so, where is the mind? I think of *mind* as the place where senses register. Sensing happens in many places: your nose, eyes, muscles, organs, brain, spinal cord, and in countless others. One of the major topics explored in this book is how your sense impressions, integral contributors to memory, are received, retained, and replayed.

For the sake of scientific description, neuroscience and psychology talk about two kinds of memory: explicit and implicit. *Explicit memory* is memory you can recall at any time and say, "I remember the time that so and so did this and that." It is also called *continuous memory. Implicit memory* is memory recalled through bodily sensations and feelings. The memory is experienced and reexperienced in the senses and can feel as though the past is happening in the present. A good example of implicit memory is the feeling you get when you again smell the odor that was in the air at the time of the original event. A familiar sensation washes over you, taking you back to a place and time. Implicit memory is also called *discontinuous memory.*

There is some controversy over implicit memory because, if such a thing exists, it implies that you can "forget" experiences that can later be remembered. For example, until eighty-odd years ago, it was thought that babies could not perceive, let alone remember, an experience, such as their birth. Even today, some health-care professionals and most health policies are unwilling to acknowledge that babies know what is happening to them when it is happening. Acknowledging the sentience of babies might change policies across sectors; it would certainly influence what governments and corporations allow themselves to do. This book is here, in part, to facilitate that change.

It is within the world of implicit memory that awareness can become a secret to its owner. Early life-shaping experiences, both wanted and unwanted, can affect everything about you, from your brain and your body to your behavior. When you are in a supportive, caring, and slowed down environment—for example, relaxing with loved ones, in meditation, or in a therapeutic environment—not only can implicit memories spontaneously emerge but also the emotions and physical sensations that go with them. Ironically, the memory of an unwanted experience can restore to you enjoyment of living and a feeling of wholeness, even with the accompanying pain of remembering.

A Place to Begin and End: Returning to Wholeness

Almost every ancient tradition contains a concept of *unity,* an undivided or unbroken completeness between seeming unrelated entities. Although a prevalent religious or spiritual teaching, in this book, I would like you to also consider unity as a dynamic spatial concept that emphasizes neither sameness nor agreement but rather *coherence* between relating entities. Another word for unity is *wholeness,* which will be used throughout this book.

When you are a baby in your mother's womb, you know life through her: Through her you learn to what degree you are in unity with or in wholeness with life. The degree to which she feels coherent about her circumstances and surroundings influences the degree to which you do. She is your first teacher, your first Earth. Her mind, her experiences, become yours. You don't even know you are separate from her until you learn to walk nearly a year after you are born. Right from your conception, you receive signals through her. This book describes how your senses of wholeness or unity are shaped through messages from your mother and the degree to which she experiences coherence with the world she inhabits, locally and globally, in the present and historically.

You can think of your relationship with your mother as a template for relationships. You will see the relationship play out at the cellular level and at the personal and interpersonal levels. If you put many relationships together—in, say, a neighborhood, a city, or a country—you will see the composite dynamics of all the first teachings, or first Earths, of each citizen. What is it that sits between people and perpetuates cooperation (wholeness) or that leads to noncooperation (separateness)? How can a lesson that happens so early become, later, such an influential phenomenon inside an individual's health, family, and society?

Luckily, every being prefers wholeness over separateness. But often the path of learning wholeness is distracted by separateness, and later, the path to remembering wholeness becomes overgrown and less obvious. Sometimes reminders are helpful. Nature, animals, the elements, loving another person, babies, and difficult circumstances—all can cause you to remember your wholeness. And when you've completely forgotten, or when the path is really challenging, shamans, medicine people, seers, and doctors serve as path clearers or decoders for you. Being reminded you were once not separate or are of unity and wholeness is a healing moment and can come from anywhere.

Essential Nature

Another term for wholeness is *essential nature*. What is essential nature? How do you know when you feel it? I'll answer the question with another question: How do you feel when you're around a baby? Have you had the experience of a baby locking his or her gaze onto yours?

There is a surprising presence in a baby's eyes: a presence that seems to reach out into a much vaster space than you might expect its little body to house. Something uncommonly large is reflected in the wide expanse of a baby's gaze. Your essential nature, no matter your life experiences, is much like the deep vastness in a baby's gaze. You remember your essential nature when you choose to relate with already coherent beings.

Your reminder can come in the form of an insight. It can come as compassion, as the sense of reawakened love, as contented relaxation, in the form of joyfulness and playfulness, and also through grief. All beings carry these gifts that remind them of their essential nature throughout life, and babies have the power to reawaken this gift in all those around them. Reconnecting with any of these feelings reminds you of your *wholeness* and the *wholeness of all that is.*

The principles in this book are offered as possible roads back to remembering your essential nature. The accompanying research and data are included to help you see that trusting babies as powerful emissaries of essential nature can lead you back to your own wholeness.

Essential Movements

Stillness

Think of stillness as a dynamic space that, although seemingly empty, is full. All movements gain their potency to move because of the fullness of stillness. Osteopath James Jealous describes stillness as akin to the experience of being underwater in the ocean. He says, "Although the surrounding water appears empty and still, you can feel the ocean moving through you."[1] Waiting in the stillness without interrupting it is the same as sitting in faith that eventually the unknown will give way to a kind of potency that builds, eventually igniting into movement. Without dynamic stillness, life ceases. The two most elemental movements that arise from stillness are *expansion* and *contraction.*

Expansion and Contraction 1

Without movement, living ceases. Think of expansion and contraction as two detectable movements life makes as expressions of its living. The expressions of expansion and contraction are found everywhere: in and around atoms, molecules, and organelles in cells, as well as in larger living beings like worms, toads, rabbits, and even human beings. Life is breathing. You could liken these movements to a jellyfish moving with the current underwater. *Your* entire body and its components also expand and contract continually, with intermittent pauses in stillness. Expansion and contraction combined with cycles of stillness have billions of ways to be expressed.

You can think of a movement, like expansion, as an *impulse,* and contraction as another impulse. When enough expressions of life or *impulses* gather together in a coordinated way, phenomena like plant growth, childbirth, sunshine, and a baby's gaze occur. Even the world turning is an organized collection of impulses. Although you most notice movement, stillness is also an impulse—one long impulse.

Both expansion and contraction are movements essential to living, and both contribute to how life expresses itself. Other examples are the freezing and thawing of water, breathing, and the surges accompanying giving birth.

Expansion and Contraction 2

The second type of expansion–contraction sets the foundation for most of the concepts in this book and has a slightly different meaning than the first type. In this second case, expansion is synonymous with growth, safety, and life-promoting circumstances. Contraction is synonymous with self-protection, fear, or life-threatening circumstances.

An earthworm provides a fascinating example of both types of expansion–contraction. To orient yourself to the first type, take yourself back to a time as long ago as your childhood. Did you ever watch a worm out on the sidewalk or in the mud of a garden or lawn expanding and contracting and writhing, wet and slimy in its bliss? Worms have a long, tubular body designed to move food through. They have a mouth at one end and an anus at the other, and you might say that life organizes the worm's impulses around eating. The worm moves to eat and eats to move. It expands and reaches with its mouth for food, then contracts to bring its body along to meet its mouth. This first memory you have of the worm shows how expansion–contraction is a normal, life-sustaining principle.

Now think of the second type of expansion–contraction. In your memory of the worm, did you ever, as a child, in your rush of curiosity, go to touch the worm's long, tubular body while it was reaching into expansion? What did it do? It recoiled. The worm, to preserve its life, contracted, becoming smaller, tighter, and less visible. Every living being knows how to expand and contract. And when needed for survival, all living beings know how to contract pronouncedly.

So what follows is that your worm, like all living beings, has two modes. It responds to two types of signals:

- Life promoting. Signals from the environment that say, "Yes, it is beneficial to expand, reach, grow, and express life." When the environment cues your worm with these signals, impulses free-flow through your worm's body, and it effortlessly expands and contracts. You could say that life-promoting signals also promote *thriving.*

- Life threatening. Signals from the environment that say, "No, it is not safe. Contract, shorten, shrink, and conceal expressions of life." When the environment cues your worm with these signals, impulses are curtailed or interrupted, making your worm retreat and become inconspicuous, shielded from danger. You could say that life-threatening signals promote *survival.* What if your worm came into contact with life-threatening signals while it was first growing and learning to move? Would it ever know how to fully expand?

This book addresses the effect that long-standing contraction, of the second type of expansion–contraction, has on babies, children, adults, and societies as a whole. It decodes the source of survival-type habits and shows how we can move toward thriving, both individually and as societies. Your worm, although without words to say it, may attest that living life by surviving is very different from living by thriving. Surviving might take more energy, nutrients, or effort. Organisms that cycle through expansion and contraction live a very different existence than those that become stuck in contraction.

All beings on this planet, whether living in trees or the trees themselves, whether swimming in oceans or the ocean's edges themselves, whether walking the earth or flying in the air, are guided in this way, by life expressing itself as impulses, informed by and possibly informing the conditions and lives that came before. This book is a starting point to explore, discern, and maybe even repair or, better yet, prevent long-standing contraction. And even though long-standing contraction is a natural part of the living world, I am fascinated by the idea that we might be able to mitigate the contractive effects that less-than-optimal early experiences have on humans and, in turn, on the rest of the planet.

In the next section, I describe how all this relates to you and the process by which your habits have formed. Later, you will be able to apply everything you read to decoding your habits.

The Mechanisms

As we look into the background of the first principle—that babies remember their experiences—we've given some thought to how life is expressed in living beings, taking the form of expansion, contraction, and stillness, which are foundational layers of movement.

In this section, we explore how those movements organize into recognizable patterns. Why? These next three major concepts—*sequencing, imprinting,* and *recapitulation*—have been grouped together by one of my mentors, Ray Castellino (and his colleagues Peter Levine and William Emerson), make up the foundation for interpreting almost every pattern that life creates, from the simple to the complex, from the linear to the spiral. For the purposes of this book, these three concepts help explain how experiences that took place when you were a newborn baby or even earlier—when you were a fetus, embryo, or cluster of cells—can still be recognized in your adult self.

Sequencing

Sequencing describes the quality of how subsequent moments are strung together. Imagine a bike chain: The shape and qualities of each link in the chain will determine what it feels like when you ride the bike. The loop can be broken down into stages. You can move in close and look at each link on its own, or you can pan out and see the links strung together as a whole chain, as a loop. The fluidity with which the sequence loops is important. If you've ever ridden a bike with a well-oiled chain, you've experienced the seamlessness of the ride: smooth. If your bike chain is rusted, or if one of the links is missing a screw, you feel it in your ride as a rough spot each time that segment of the chain comes through. All sequences have unique characteristics in which one phase may be different from another.

Tree growth has a sequence, brushing your teeth is a sequence, and long-term projects, like growing a business or forming a relationship, are sequences. Imagine that expansion–contraction of your first cell has a sequence, as do your first heartbeat and your first movement in the womb. From where do the influences that shape your sequences arise? Your mother? Your father? Your genes? The human genome? Your environment? When you think about it, the number of possibilities is immense. Clusters of cells come together, and their combined sequencing will shape the sequence of an organ. The organ will pulse, react, and disperse enzymes and hormones as dictated by the composite sequencing of its cells. Gradually, a whole person will move, respond, and live as an orchestra of sequences. Even personality is a mosaic of sequences.

Later, we explore how sequencing is subject to influences from your mother, your father, and the prevailing social norms when you were conceived, as well as influences from your parents' parents and the societal norms of *their* times, and so on. In the second half of this book, you learn about a process called *intuitive recovery,* which will help you illuminate patterns in your sequencing by peering into the window of your early prebirth and birth experiences. You will work backward along this powerful sight line, decoding your sequencing so you can make out the shape your early experiences have left. Before that, though, we will look at another aspect called *imprinting*.

Imprinting

An *imprint* is the lasting effect a positive or challenging event or circumstance has on any living being, human or otherwise. We will concentrate on the imprints that come from challenging circumstances. This type of imprint forms when the power of the life-threatening signal is greater than your power to discharge its effects. In other words, if you can adequately shake off, run from, decompress from, cry over, get angry about, or do whatever you need to do to resolve a large, uncomfortable surprise, you likely will not be imprinted by the experience. However, as long as the life-threatening signal continues transmitting, the contraction will not resolve. And sometimes, if you have been unable to respond to a signal or discharge its effects, the contraction will continue even after the signal stops.

An imprint is the result of unresolved contractions from an overwhelming or life-threatening message. When you have been imprinted, your body behaves as though the life-threatening signal is continuing even after the original signal has stopped.

Imprints shape sequencing, as the sequence takes on the shape, tone, and depth of the imprint. Think of an imprint as similar to the dent in your car after a car crash. You can look at the dent, estimate the size of the vehicle that hit it, the color of the car (if there is any paint left in the dent), and maybe even how long ago the accident happened, based on the rust in the dent.

Here's another way of looking at imprints, which shows how they play out over time. A stone falls in the river. As soon as the stone's presence is added to the river bed, water must flow around it. The change starts as minute shifts in water flow, and over time the silt and debris carried downstream collect on the front lip of the stone. Water is diverted further around the tiny mound, so the pile of debris grows larger. Sure enough, after a few years the shape and direction of the river has changed as a result of what once was only a tiny stone.

You and your body respond to imprints much as a river does. Your essential nature is never touched by imprints, but they can overlay your essential nature, affecting your inner and outer being and making it appear as though they are you. The source of the imprint, like the source of the dent in your car, can be traced by examining your sequencing, working back through the evidence. Sequencing is the look of the car after the impact. The imprint is the force, circumstances, and storyline behind the dent. The experiences of all living things are recorded or imprinted and are detectable in their sequencing.

Later, in Chapter 5, the chapter dealing with the Intuitive Recovery Project (IRP), you learn how to identify and dissipate imprints in your sequencing. But first, how are imprints identified?

Imprints in Your Body

Imprints sit like rocks along the river of your nerves' impulses. In the first few weeks after your exposure to the life-threatening signal, the imprint is loose and pliable, like light sand. You can easily dissipate it if you have the chance to tell your story and be understood by another. By recounting the story, or through body-centered therapy, or even simply by being able to react naturally, in an animal way, by shaking, biting, fighting, or fleeing, you can ensure the event does not make a lasting impression on you.

However, if the power of the impulse to discharge the signal is overwhelmed by the strength of the signal, your body will absorb an imprint. Think of it as a repressed shake, bite, fight, or flight. If you haven't had the chance to respond, or to respond adequately, the signal will leave a mark or a habit that will mimic the force, its vector, and the degree of restraint you had to impose on your emotional response at the time you were overwhelmed. Immediately, and over time, the affected area of your body will accentuate the habits resonating with and from that experience.

The imprint may appear as unexplainable deadened or accentuated sensations or as decreased mobility. Your skin may be a slightly different tone in that area. That area of your body may get less or more blood circulation. Imprints are often unresponsive to diet, stretching, and exercise. They may respond a little, but when you stop, the area is quick to return to its usual state.

How do you detect an imprint? It may be a place in your body that you don't like or that you wish were "different." Notice how you think of that area. Innocently, you may treat the area as a failure, or with a sense of futility, a feeling that it will "never change" or that it is "just how it is." Maybe you even feel like your body has betrayed you. This is common. Every time you touch that part of your body, you may feel irritated, or you may promise to change it. What you may never have considered is that these unsettled feelings derive from an imprint. The critical sensation might actually be coming from a "rock" sitting in your sequence's "river," or from "the circumstance" behind "your dent." Try replacing your judgment with compassion. Be relentless. Notice what starts to happen.

Imprints in Your Personality

The body is not the only place you'll notice imprints. They also manifest in your personality and in your emotional responses. In these cases, the imprint expresses itself as a disproportionately large or seemingly illogical response to a present circumstance. For example, your friend tells you his leg is hurting, and you feel bad about it, as though you had a role in creating his pain. Feeling culpable for the pain of another may be rooted in prebirth or birth experiences. Often a baby who gestated in the womb of a mother who lacked the support to comfortably concentrate on the life growing inside her can feel responsible for that lack.

People spend years in counseling, hoping to change or understand their emotional response patterns. But because the imprint is walled off, protected from conscious awareness, strictly intellectual inquiries may not access it. Understanding the imprint intellectually may be an important step in changing resonance with the imprint, but feeling the emotion of an imprint that has never had the opportunity to be felt often frees you from resonating with it as strongly. To explain further, the irrationally large or seemingly unrelated emotion you experience under certain circumstances is very similar to the feelings you couldn't afford to have at the time you took on the imprint. Because it was too overwhelming for you then, your body intelligently whisked it away from your attention. You can still resonate with your essential nature sometimes, but if just the right number of circumstances arises—for example, if you're tired, haven't eaten well, and are triggered in the present by a circumstance that is similar to that which caused the imprint—the emotions that accompanied the imprint may play out. This is called *recapitulation,* and you will learn about that next.

All living beings are imprinted. All living beings know how to dissipate imprints. The last part of the book focuses on how it is never too late to repair an imprint.

Recapitulation

Recapitulation describes what happens when an event plays out with uncannily similar physical postures, behaviors, emotions, and even circumstances as the original, challenging, imprinting life experience. When you are confronted with an environment that is similar to the one that first led to an imprint, it's as if a "play" button has been pressed on a recording, and even though the tune seems unfamiliar, somehow you know the steps of the dance and, to your surprise, perform rather well. Although not an exact repeat, it is as though an imprint has you perceiving and possibly even attracting circumstances similar to those of the past. Sometimes you're not even aware it's happening until after it's finished, although a clue that it's happening could be that you feel compelled to do something that you realize is self-destructive.

Recapitulation as a Self-Righting Mechanism

It all sounds quite ominous, doesn't it? It's as if you are being hypnotized and led around by some malevolent force. Reading about imprints and recapitulation can feel overwhelming. You might be asking, "Why do I keep doing this? Shouldn't I have this figured out by now?" Try this reframing: What if recapitulation, the replaying of an imprint, is actually part of the design to heal the imprint? What if, somehow, replaying the circumstances and themes of the original challenging life circumstance is life's funny way of directing you back to your wholeness and back to your essential nature?

A recapitulation can be an uncomfortable sensation you get when you feel a certain part of your body. It can be an emotional response you have to certain news even though no one else can relate to its magnitude. It can be a restlessness, as in the case of Mark, whom you will soon read about. He kept moving homes and changing jobs until he discovered his imprint was one of the roots of his challenges.

Because recapitulations are so uncomfortable, they can be distracting. Sometimes it's hard to have the wherewithal to ask the compassionate question, "Where is this habit arising from?" It can sometimes take a long time to recognize that a recapitulation is, in fact, a pattern replaying from an earlier time and not simply a grievous and random set of circumstances playing out in the present. Sometimes imprints and recapitulations are so uncomfortable that you are compelled to do something about them. When you and people like Mark discover there are reasons seemingly incurable present-day habits form, you gain renewed empowerment, and with compassionate awareness around recapitulation, the imprint can be transformed.

Case Study: Mark

Mark was thirty years old when he first came for a session. Besides his physical complaints of not being able to sleep well and having a general sense of "irritation" when he was in small spaces or when people touched him, he also shared that he would sometimes wake up feeling like he couldn't breathe. He recounted what he knew about how he came into the world. He was told that he was conceived despite his mother having an IUD (a contraceptive device worn in the uterus that prevents the development of pregnancy). He was also born prematurely and spent his first few weeks of life outside the womb in an incubator.

While we worked together, locating areas of restriction in his body (mainly his head and lungs), Mark began to remember a palpable irritation and near panic as he remembered an "irritating metallic feeling" above the right side of his head. What Mark came to realize was that the

IUD he shared his mother's womb with had essentially been "looming over" him, threatening his life. Because it was designed to prevent a baby from growing, he had to stay as alert as possible so that he could "hold on" to his life for the first trimester of his growth. Now, even at the age of thirty, Mark was recapitulating the irritation and the fear for his safety.

I encouraged him to feel the stability presented to him in the treatment room and to let his body resonate with this new and real experience while simultaneously remembering his original learning. Mark found it hard to trust stability because staying in one place long enough to gain stability in his original world would have led to his death. Thus there was no stability in his early environment, and if he wanted to survive, trusting and relaxing would have been fatal. Although he had survived, the imprint of the IUD recapitulated every day in his irritability and difficulty sleeping. It was as though Mark remembered his impending death, not to mention his parents' inadvertent ambiguity about him, every day.

Eventually, however, the more stable sensation resonated with his essential nature, and Mark's system gradually began attuning to stability. He didn't have to give up his ability to stay alert, but he could experiment with trust. After he realized that no one had ever offered him empathy for how vulnerable he felt in his mother's womb, he could finally experience grief. He also felt profound grief for how hard he had been working to avoid impending deathlike feelings his whole life. Although it was painful at that moment to take inventory of how vulnerable and scared he had been as a prenate, he soon noticed the deep pleasure and delight he felt at his ability to move without irritation and to take full breaths without anxiety. He worked for several months, both one-on-one and in a group, before sleep came easily. The impulse in his nervous system was no longer interrupted by the imprint of his mother's IUD. His essential nature began to reemerge, manifesting as trust that he would not die if he was still and/or close to people.

An interesting note about Mark is that he consistently arrived early for his sessions. After several months, I found him arriving on time. When I shared this observation with Mark, he laughed. He not only had been recapitulating the irritation from the IUD in his mother's uterus but had been recapitulating his premature birth too.

The Model

How long have science and medicine treated the roots of illness as belonging solely to the individual and to the individual's present? Although they concede a person's ailment may be caused by environmental and genetic factors, they do not study it in the context of the person's family and community. What if, when you are unsettled or ill, you do not have a physical problem but are reacting to your ecology, within and without? What if babies, when they are unsettled or ill, not only are responding to physical issues but are also trying to express important information that might benefit everyone? How would you treat yourself and others if you felt this was true?

This is the perspective put forward by the *family field* model. This model is not new. It is a modern-day echo of the spirit of many intact sacred healing traditions from around the world; Japanese, Chinese, Indian, and Polynesian traditions, to name a few, share the family field tenet, which is to be in right relationship with all that is, both seen and unseen. What concepts must we explore to understand what this means, and how does it relate to babies, their families, and society?

Fields

> Fields are invisible organizing regions of influence just like magnets. Matter arises from Fields rather than Fields arising from matter.
>
> **—Rupert Sheldrake, "Morphic Resonance" workshop, Hollyhock Retreat Center, July 2009**

The family field model describes how familial and societal traits can express in a baby's health. When biologist Rupert Sheldrake says that "matter arises from fields rather than fields arising from matter," he means that a composite of habits (field) exists before your body (matter) does, and informs your body's shape as it is coming into existence. Consequently, your form also informs the field as you come into being. The preexisting habits are a composite of all like beings that came before you, with your blood relatives being the most influential.

The fields that inform embryonic development, whether for humans, rats, rabbits, or horses, are called *morphogenetic fields.* The concept of morphogenetic fields was first introduced by Alexander Gurwitsch in 1910. Because the family field model explores not only morphogenetic fields (i.e., embryological development) but also the influences family and society have on your present-day health, two of the best scientific explanations for the model are discussed next: *morphic resonance* and *epigenetics.* These two theories challenge the genetic determinacy view that has been popular since the 1930s, which says that cellular development and physical traits are informed only by your genes.

First, though, before we look at how fields can affect babies, families, and societies, you need a sense of what fields are and how they relate to you. Start big: Earth has an electromagnetic field around it. There is a positive pole and a negative pole, just as there are on a battery. The field created between and around the two poles is measureable, and it fluctuates.[2] Similarly, there are electromagnetic fields, like the ones surrounding the earth, around all living beings. The body has a measureable electromagnetic field, as do every one of your organs. And fields can affect other fields. For example, exposure to other fields can potentially alter the shape and frequency of your human energy field, which is why it is recommended that you avoid living close to power lines and that you protect your body from cell phones.

What if you went a little further and imagined that emotions and thoughts had fields? Have you ever wondered what it is you sense when you walk by someone and are drawn to him—or are repelled or even disturbed by his presence? Or maybe you have had the experience of knowing the mood of your partner, roommate, or child when she came into the room, even before you have seen or spoken to her. What were you sensing at a distance? Perhaps it was his emotional field.

You don't even have to be close to the person to register a sense of her. The field that the human heart creates has been registered at least a meter from the body,[3] which is why an electrocardiogram (ECG) normally reads the body with electrodes and can also be accurately read off the body.[4] The signal is weaker but readable.

Morphic Resonance and Patterns of Inheritance

Drawing on the scientific concepts of morphogenetic fields, contemporary biologist Rupert Sheldrake developed his theory of *morphic resonance,* which proposes that an individual's physical and behavioral attributes are not solely the result of inherited genes but are also influenced by "resonance" between individuals of previous generations of similar life forms. Sheldrake also suggests that the most closely related beings of the same species in space and time have the greatest influence on the next generation.[5] What this means is that you share the most resonance with your parents because they came most recently before you. Your body and behavior will resonate the most with theirs. You also have resonance with your great-great-grandparents but less than you do with your parents. Although Sheldrake does not specify this, the family field suggests that you have resonance with the society surrounding you at the time you are born as well as with the society's trends. You have resonance with the society into which your great-great-grandparents were born too but less than you do with the one into which your parents were born.

Sheldrake bases his theory on Michael Faraday's nineteenth-century concepts of electromagnetic fields,[6] on formative causation, and on twentieth-century research in developmental biology. He states, "For understanding development, genes and gene products are not enough. Morphogenesis [embryonic development] also depends on organizing fields."[7]

So how do fields and resonance with fields organize your development? Picture any kind of field as an invisible wind. The wind has blown around, picked up, and now carries qualities from many variables, including the time and place of your parents' and grandparents'; the quality of the air, food, and water around your mother before and while she was conceiving you; the quality of the relationship between your parents; their motivations for bringing you into the world; and the existing cultural climate at the time. And then you come and encounter that wind, are shaped by it, and impress your signature on it as well.

The study of *epigenetics,* which literally means "above the genes," also shows how inheritance comes from the environment as well as from genes. Influences like chemicals, electricity, and hormones (which include emotions, because body chemistry and emotions reflect each other) direct which genes are expressed in a developing baby.[8] The environment literally signals to the genes which ones should "turn on" and which can stay "switched off."[9]

The Family Field

The family field model builds on the ideas of morphic resonance and epigenetics to explain the composite set of influences acting on babies when they are conceived and gestating. The influences continue throughout life but have their most significant influence in utero and at birth because of rapid growth at those times. The model shows the way imprints are inherited from previous generations and from society, and it shows how the imprints babies have may relate to experiences that did not originate with them.

In the family field model, the past can influence the present as though it is happening in the present. For example, your grandparents may have had to flee the country they were born in, and there may have been difficult circumstances like leaving other family members, experiencing disease, watching deaths happen, or starvation. Most migratory people have stories like this somewhere in their ancestry. If those grandparents, because their focus was on moving forward and surviving, never grieved the challenges they faced at that time, the field in which they conceived their children would likely have resonance with those difficulties. There would be an unspoken imprint in the grandparents' wind that would become part of the composite, informing wind of their child. That child, your parent—let's say your mother—would exhibit resonance of some kind with your grandparents' experiences. Maybe she would also not speak of challenges arising in her life. Maybe she would have a certain lean to her posture that resembles the posture of one of your grandparents.

This may sound similar to just saying, "My parent 'learned' to be that way because my grandparent 'modeled' it." But morphic resonance, epigenetics, and the family field suggest that the learned behavior is not as simple as "I see, therefore I do," and the body posture is not as simple as "it's genetic." The difference in *resonance* vs. *inheritance* is that resonance can change. To this end, the family field also explores how to repair the effects of the past on present-day physical and emotional symptoms in babies, children, and adults.

Objects in the Field

The previous section describes how ancestors, groups, or societies imprint individuals in the present. An *object in the field* is the composite "shape" or complex that arises when you combine all the individuals, both past and present, who resonate with a common imprint. Individuals in the object could include people that share blood lines or societies. In other words, an imprint can be inherited from a time before an individual's birth or conception and has potentially been perpetuated by multiple individuals over generations. For all intents and purposes, objects in the field are imprints, but the more specific term describes the resonance an imprint has across multiple individuals in space and time. Although they are perceivably from another time, objects operate as though they exist in the present day. They are also dynamic; when viewed spatially, they behave like a fluctuating constellation or as a sort of "dressing" on top of the essential natures of the people related to each other or to a shared experience.

Descendants of Holocaust survivors or of victims of war crimes or sexual abuse have been known to resonate with their parents' or grandparents' imprints, even though they did not live through the events themselves.[10] Like imprints, objects in the field are the result when the strength of a life-threatening signal overwhelms an individual's or a population's ability to discharge it. Objects in the field can be the result of events or circumstances endured by entire cultures at once: famine, poverty, and war, for instance, or environmental challenges like low air quality, lack of food, environmental disasters, and water pollution. Objects affect individuals and their concurrent and subsequent cultures.

Now, if you haven't already, bring this idea back to you. When parents are preparing to conceive, their conception field resonates most closely with information and experiences in their immediate family field. Depending on your spiritual and religious beliefs, you may recognize that there are many variables creating the directives that determine a baby's growth, such as the Hindu belief of Karma.[11] You may also think about children you know who, although displaying a family resemblance in appearance and behavior, also possess qualities and personality traits unlike those of any member of their immediate family. The implication is that over and above the parents' gene pool, their preexisting emotional, chemical, and historical climates, as well as those of their grandparents and their societies, will influence which traits are encouraged in the baby.

It is a fascinating theory: In order to enter this world successfully and survive the journey from preconception through the first birthday, children must take direction from the preexisting objects established by their family, their ancestors, and their family's and ancestors' societal environments.[12] Why would this be? What is the benefit of similarity?

Perhaps if babies can achieve a high degree of compatibility with their family and society, they will be better recognized as belonging to that family and that society. Belonging encourages survival, so it is understandable why resonance with the family field is immediately required. For reasons of survival and belonging, and even for the eventual fulfillment of life purpose, it makes sense that babies are extremely adept at blending into and adapting to their surroundings.

Identifying Objects in the Field

Observing your imprints, or your present-day challenges, is the first step to identifying the objects in the field that you are recapitulating. Evidence of them is found in your posture, in your emotional responses to stress, in your style of intimacy, and in your internal physiology. Because an object can be likened to elaborate webbing that threads through, and is suspended between, a group of people related by blood, experience, or shared beliefs, there is no limit to how far back in time a family field extends. There is also no limit to how widely it may reach across societies.

Medicine brilliantly diagnoses and treats babies, and indeed all humans, through its lens of "disorder" or "disease." It is true that objects in the field, although not exclusively physical in their manifestations, can appear as physical symptoms and can be relieved through a medical diagnosis and treatment. However, many other health challenges are unchanged by medical treatment because individuals, including babies, are diagnosed apart from their family field, and treatment begins and ends in the physical realm only. Treating the objects in the family field relieves pressure on you and on anyone related to the object, affording greater clarity and a right relationship with all living beings, both seen and unseen. Using the family field makes it impossible to perceive any one's symptoms to be a result of having something "wrong" with them. Treatment effectively, and without blame, addresses the historical threads linked to your or your baby's symptoms.

In the following case study, you will see how using the family field model takes the emphasis off a baby "having a problem" and instead focuses on extending medicine in the form of empathy (among other things) to her and the family field.

Case Study: Anne's Family

In this case study, a family noticed the baby's symptoms, or recapitulation, and in the course of exploring the roots of these symptoms, inadvertently transformed the health of their whole family.

Following a seminar I presented, Anne asked me to work with her family. She told me she had hemorrhaged after the birth of her daughter four months earlier and had nearly died. She felt the family was still recovering from the trauma and knew that, in some way, her baby daughter must have been affected. She asked if I would work with them, and I committed to her. She also asked me if Jacqueline, her fourteen-year-old daughter from her previous marriage, could join the session along with her husband, Jordan, and their baby, Elizabeth.

Anne said, "I think it's really important for her, and she would find it really interesting."

I said, "Sure, I think it would be great."

Ahead of our appointment, Anne filled out forms I had sent her to get a history of everyone in the family. She answered questions about whether their daughter's conception was planned, gave details of the pregnancy and the birth, and answered important questions about her own and her husband's stories as children and babies in their own families. She also filled out a form for her fourteen-year-old.

I went to their house on the day of the appointment and was met at the door by a clear- and sparkly eyed young woman, fourteen-year-old Jacqueline. I was struck by the look in her eyes. They seemed to say, "I am the girl I was born to be, and I'm proud of who I am." I was unaccustomed to seeing a young woman with a look of such knowing. I know my friends and I, as teenagers, were taught to respond to authority figures and older people with a degree of inferiority. As a result, we tended to be shy or at least mildly uncomfortable in the presence of adults and were more ourselves when with siblings or friends. So I felt comfort with, and deep appreciation for, her confidence. She welcomed me in, and we chatted about her school while Anne, Jordon, and four-month-old Elizabeth settled down in the living room with us.

Jordon spoke enthusiastically about the work we were about to do together. He and Anne had spent some time "looking into" their emotional patterns, and Jordon reiterated his interest in resolving anything that would help him live life fully in the present. I was encouraged by his openness. Anne was intrigued to discover what would happen in our session, as was I.

I had learned a great deal about the patterns in the family by reading the forms they had filled out before our visit. The following are some of the notable details:

- All during her pregnancy, Anne had the experience of "not feeling supported."
- As a family, they had moved to a different city and changed homes twice during that time.

- Anne felt Jordon had been hard on her and not as understanding as she needed.

She added that they had "worked through" a lot of it and that Jordon was "much better now."

The forms gather information about long-standing family field patterns, and when we looked farther back in Anne's early life, we could see there was an object in the field that manifested as a "lack of support" from her first husband and, even farther back, from her own father. Anne's father was physically abusive and an alcoholic, and he left her family when she was three. Anne described her prior marriage as "peaceful but unsupportive."

Another object in the family field was that this wasn't the first time Anne had hemorrhaged. A milder hemorrhage had happened after Jacqueline's birth. This was significant. When a woman feels relaxed, supported, and bonded with those around her during pregnancy, she will have high levels of the hormone oxytocin, which ensures that the blood vessels attached to the placenta will contract and close off bleeding when the placenta is expelled after birth. In contrast, when a woman does not feel supported during pregnancy, or when she experiences states of high stress, as in Anne's case, oxytocin will be in low supply, and hemorrhaging is a risk. (You will learn more about oxytocin in Chapter 2.)

I turned my attention to Elizabeth, the baby. Although her torso showed a prominent curve to the left, her eyes were bright and joyous. I knew her posture was telling me something about the family's field.

Since support had been missing from Anne's life and seemed to be an object in the field, I asked Jordon if he would be willing to sit behind Anne on the couch and have her lean on him for support. We got him comfortable and then she leaned back on his chest.

"I have a rule," I warned them. "Nobody is allowed to be polite here. Everyone needs to be comfortable and ask for pillows, move, do whatever they need so you can feel relaxed."

We spent a few minutes practicing "no politeness" and letting Anne try out being specific about her requirements for relaxation. The idea was to set them up in a position so Anne could feel support from Jordon in the way she had needed it during her pregnancy. Elizabeth would then be able to feel that support coming through Anne from her dad.

We began a game called "attachment sequencing." This is a sequence that all mammals go through after they are born, when they leave their mother's pelvis and instinctively find her nipple, latch on, suck, and swallow her milk. It is considered to be the true indicator that birth is complete. Jordon and Anne shared that Elizabeth had, in fact, self-attached in the hospital after she was born, and they had been encouraging her to do that ever since. I was thrilled to hear this. It meant that this would be easy for Elizabeth, and I might have extra time in the session to do some gentle bodywork on her.

We began by placing the baby on Anne's hips. I asked Jacqueline if she would be interested in participating. She agreed, although I could see that some of the ease in her face had changed to tension. I slowed down and mentally took note of the change. Going ahead, Jacqueline and I placed our hands under Elizabeth's feet so she could push off our hands as she made her way up Anne's belly toward her breast. We all gently encouraged her to find her way. She began to wriggle and move up, as all babies do. Not ten seconds into her journey, however, I watched a long wavelike shudder travel from the center of Elizabeth's body, out to the top of her head and down to her feet, followed by sudden crying.

The face of every family member changed when this happened. We stopped, brought Elizabeth to Anne's breast, and let her nurse to soothe herself. Both Anne and Jordon were quick to note that Elizabeth had not had trouble prior to this time and had not had trouble when going through her attachment sequence. They weren't sure what was going on. I had the sense that Elizabeth was telling us where in her sequence she had experienced an imprint. We all decided that once Elizabeth had calmed down, we would try attachment sequencing again.

Again, on the second try, in the exact same spot as before, Elizabeth seemed to get stuck, become frustrated, and begin crying. We stopped again and moved Elizabeth back to Anne's chest. I did a quick check around the family, and that was when I noticed that Jacqueline was in tears.

"It's a lot, isn't it?" I asked her quietly.

She nodded, wiping her eyes, without making eye contact.

"Yeah," she said. "It is a lot." I knew only she knew what "it" was.

She looked at her mother and then at all of us and said, "You know, when you were in the hospital, and I had to go to school every day, I was walking around the halls thinking my mom might die, and it felt so weird not to be able to tell anyone and to try to be normal. It just wasn't normal!" And she cried deeply while Anne leaned in as if to say, "I'm listening. I'm here now."

Through sobs, Jacqueline continued, "I didn't want to tell anyone! Because I didn't want to take more of your energy away from you; you were already so weak! I thought if I tell you, then it might make things worse! That it would kill you."

Anne reached to hold Jacqueline, with Elizabeth happily folded into her body, sleeping quietly.

It felt clear, then, that Jacqueline's effort to protect her mom from her own feelings so as not to deplete her might have been a habit she learned way back at the time of her own birth, when she sensed Anne was unavailable because she was hemorrhaging. Because "lack of support" was already an object in the field long before Jacqueline came to be, she may have been grieving a loss that belonged to her mother and possibly others before her.

I said, "I have a feeling that this might have been what it was like when you came into the world."

Jacqueline looked in my eyes as babies often do when something true is said. She didn't answer me but joined her baby sister and folded into her mother's arms while Jordon supported them all.

I continued, "Thank you for telling me all these feelings you were having. It really was a lot to go through."

After sharing a few moments with her baby sister, resting in her mother's arms, Jacqueline lifted her tear-stained face and turned to look at us. She said, "At first, I didn't know what I was doing here, why I needed to be here. When we started doing the attachment sequencing, I thought to myself, 'This is stupid!' Then all these feelings came over me that I didn't even know were there." She laughed, and we all laughed with her, then talked some more about what it was like for her to go through that week when she almost lost her mom.

After some time, we agreed the session felt like it was ending. They stayed together on the couch as I gently pulled away from them. I left the house quietly and closed the door behind me.

The next day, Anne and I had an opportunity to follow up about the session. She said, "After you left, we just stayed on the couch together, snuggling. It must have been twenty minutes or so. It was so nice. That night, Jacqueline decided she wanted to sleep in the bed with us, so we all piled in together. We slept so deeply. Even Elizabeth slept through the night, and she never does! And we couldn't believe it when we woke up. I turned to look at Elizabeth, and her eyes were open, and she was smiling right into my face. And then, after watching her struggle to use her arms for months, she began moving them in a way that she never had before. She'd been having trouble reaching, she just wasn't interested, and there she was, using both arms, reaching out and back!"

We both sat there with tears in our eyes, knowing Anne had watched something very special unfold. They all had been holding a piece of the family field. When Jacqueline was able to clear her piece of it, Elizabeth was able to more fully inhabit her growing edge. They had been operating like one organism, as families do, and the object in the family field had been influencing all their experiences. We all bore witness to the magical, intimate, and powerful dynamic of a whole system.

It wasn't long before this event that I had been treating babies' health conditions as symptoms specific to them. Although thorough, my education had not prepared me to include parents, and society in general, in a child's health profile. After slowly giving myself permission, over the space of years, to respond to what I was seeing rather than what I was taught to see, my practice has turned me into a fresh student of families and babies. I continue to be astounded and comforted that the families I work with contain within them everything I need to know. In the right environment, they reveal their family field, which contains all the necessary ingredients to take them to their next natural step.

Perspectives and Purposes

Even though babies, especially in their first month of development in the womb, are responding to the fields of their parents and their parents' environment, in no way should you or others feel guilt or a sense of "wrongdoing" if you unknowingly affect them. Unless you truly did do something wrong (in which case, apologies are always helpful), innocent mistakes are one of the most natural aspects of being human. And the resulting imprints can be used as handholds to transform you, your family, and your society, providing all with great fulfillment. Humans seem to be designed to face and overcome difficulty. It's exciting to consider that your habits may not simply be "genetic" and that you may be able to change the ones that are harmful or restrictive.

It's also exciting to consider that you can assert some degree of influence over whether you carry on your family's and society's traditions (like this family's example of "feeling unsupported").

You serve all by doing the work that is offered in this book, and the work that human beings are doing, with or without this book, serves you. It is never too late to repair your imprints. You will not change history, but you can alter your response to the memory of how it influences your sequencing. You can shift society and the effect of history on future generations.

In the following chapters, you learn about examples of objects in art, music, language, medicine, addiction, suicide, and even in the discovery of the "new world."

Summary

Expansion and contraction are the two primary movements after stillness. All living beings possess the ability to expand and contract. Life-promoting signals encourage all beings to reach and expand, followed by a contraction. Under life-promoting circumstances, this cycle repeats with equal intensity in both directions, and all beings thrive when in this cycle. Under life-threatening signals, living beings contract so they are inconspicuous. Beings in this cycle are simply surviving.

All beings' impulses organize into recognizable patterns or sequences. The qualities of a sequence are informed by many variables, most notably the earliest period of development, which for babies is from preconception through the first month of gestation. Imprinting is the phenomenon that occurs when the impulse from a life-threatening signal is stronger than the living being's power to discharge it. Imprints will reveal themselves in the sequence as recapitulations—remnant recordings of original life-threatening signals that are wrongly attributed to present circumstances.

The central tenet of the family field is that there is a web of resonance between like beings. You are connected to all living beings through the myriad qualities you share, be they your essential nature or your imprints. When you view babies and your health through the lens of the family field, you identify two impulses: your essential nature and its natural radiance shining out from under imprints and objects in the family field and recapitulations of your own, your family's, and your society's imprints, past and present, referred to as objects in the field.

The family field is a paradigm and healing model that diagnoses and treats present-day symptoms in the context of your prebirth and birth periods and the lives, prebirth, and birth periods of your parents, as well as those of your more distant ancestors and all the societies surrounding you and those before you. Treating objects in the field can resolve health symptoms in babies, their families, and society in general.

CHAPTER 2

The Second Principle

Consciousness Precedes the Brain Architecture That Supports It

We know that the baby is far more sophisticated than anything we ever gave it credit for being before. We didn't think it could have an experience, we didn't think it could sense anything, and we didn't think it had the brains to know what the senses were telling them. The mind does not develop like the brain develops. The mind is just a part of who they are, and that's a new idea.

—David Chamberlain, PhD, "What Babies Are
Teaching Us about Violence"

When Dr. Akira Ikegawa, director of the Ikegawa OB/GYN clinic in Yokohama, Japan, was conducting routine interviews with children, he began hearing accounts from patients under five years old about their own conceptions, gestations, and births.[1] Intrigued by his accidental discovery, he decided to formalize a questionnaire, which he then administered to seventy-nine children, publishing the results in the book *I Remember When I Was in Mommy's Tummy*. Compelled further by those results, he interviewed more than 3,500 children about the same topic. What he consistently found was that over 30 percent of the children who answered the survey had prebirth memories and 20 percent remembered parts of their birth. Here is an excerpt from his second book on the topic, *I Chose You to Be My Mommy*:

> *It was dark inside Mommy's tummy, but it was warm, and I was swimming. I couldn't wait to see Mommy.*
>
> *When I was born, it was too bright. When it's time to be born, somebody will let you know: "Now you can go." I couldn't wait for Mommy to hold me (in her arms). But I was in a glass box.*
>
> *Mother's commentary*: "From the time he started to talk until he was about four years old, he used to tell me this all the time. I was surprised because he couldn't have known that he had been in an infant incubator for several hours after his birth."[2]

Because the earliest period of life is preverbal (before words), you will find that the memory of it is not always stored in explicit, or conscious, memory. Rather, it is stored in implicit or nonconscious memory. Many of the children Ikegawa talked to would not have been able to recall their experiences because they were in implicit memory and therefore not in the realm of conversation (although, obviously, some children do retain the information in their explicit memory). Ikegawa suggests that the number of children and adults who retain content from their early experiences in their implicit memory is actually much higher, perhaps 100 percent. How is this possible? Understanding this biological paradox begins with an overview of how the brain develops.

The Biological Paradox

The family field model suggests that events occurring early in pregnancy and, even before conception, influence how your brain, behaviors, and bonds form. This statement is paradoxical because, even today, many people, including health professionals working in obstetrics, believe that babies can't have an experience, let alone remember it. If objects in the field influence the development of present generations, this suggests that consciousness must precede the brain structures originally thought to support it. Consciousness itself has no universally recognized definition, and rather than trying to define it here, we use Rupert Sheldrake's theory of morphic resonance set out in his book *A New Science of Life* to explore how consciousness shapes form through fields.[3]

To this end, the first half of the chapter focuses on neurology—specifically *embryological neurology,* the study of brain formation in the womb. The second section focuses on biochemistry—specifically on two hormones, oxytocin and cortisol, that shape brain development, bonding, and later behaviors in children and adults. This section also examines how early addictions to these chemicals are established at birth and how this has been shown to be true for animals as well as humans.

Brains, Fields, and Development

It has long been accepted that the first three years of life dramatically shape the physiological qualities of your brain. Science is now also aware that your earliest experiences lay the groundwork for how you will develop in your first three years of life.[4] The family field model introduces the concept that your ancestors and your ancestors' environments also shape your brain. Now we will add—and explore—the idea that animals share your ancestry too.

Based on the most widely accepted medical embryology textbooks by T. W. Sadler, by eighteen days after conception, you began to form the earliest version of your nervous system.[5] Much like the worm from your childhood memory, your body started out looking like a long tube and was mostly made up of your heart. By day twenty-seven, your brain's first recognizable primitive structures—the *hindbrain,* the *midbrain,* and the *forebrain*—became visibly demarcated from one another and, surprisingly, used to wrap around your heart.[6] At day thirty-two, these regions differentiated again and gave rise to the rest of your brain structures.

Going back to day eighteen again, if you could watch brain development as though it were a movie, you would see how out of your hindbrain awakens what is known as the oldest part of the brain. In neuroanatomy, *old* means something is older than the advent of humans, amphibians, and reptiles. The *reptilian brain* first appeared on the planet five hundred million years ago in prehistoric fish. It further evolved when reptiles arrived, and it was named for them, aptly, as you'll read later.

Later in embryological development, during the second trimester, the second-oldest structure emerges. This is the *limbic system,* which grows out of the midbrain and appears to fit perfectly on top of the reptilian brain. Another name for the limbic system is the *old mammalian brain,* which commemorates the first living creatures to possess it: small mammals. The limbic system arrived on the planet 150 million years ago.

In the third trimester, the *neocortex* (otherwise known as the *new mammalian brain*) develops. This advanced part of the brain first appeared two or three million years ago, with the development of the *Homo* genus. The neocortex humans have today arrived only 150,000 years ago, with *Homo sapiens.* The neocortex is the collection of dense folds you see when you look at a brain from the outside.

And development doesn't stop there. The brain continues differentiating even after birth, when the anthropologically newest, and therefore most evolved, part of the brain emerges: the prefrontal lobes. Humans and apes are the only known Earth-based species to achieve this level of brain differentiation, with humans certainly being the largest.[7]

Each level of the brain governs different functions of living, from the simple acts of breathing, eating, and sleeping to the functions of higher reason and compassion. It is interesting that, as the human brain develops, it follows the same path in months that evolution followed over millennia. Consecutive stages of human nervous system development mirror the systems belonging to species that preceded humans, from the simplest to the more complex. This means that when you began as a *conceptus* (a union of sperm and egg), you resembled the first single-cell organisms on this planet. At every stage you resonate with the species most similar to your stage of development, and you are informed by the ever-more complex resonance from species that succeeded the first cell.

Another interesting and vital point is that how well each level of the brain functions is, in part, determined by how well preceding levels developed and functioned.[8] The levels do not function separately from one another. Rather, they collaborate in endless feedback circuits among themselves in a cooperative synchrony.

For example, some learning disabilities, hearing or comprehension impairments, and vision disturbances are not actually caused by damage to the nerves of the cerebral cortex, the ears, or the eyes, but are in fact the result of disruptions in the working of either the limbic system or the reptilian brain.[9] Because the limbic system is developing during the second trimester of pregnancy and the reptilian brain during the first trimester, the successful function of the completely developed brain at birth depends on how well the early stages of pregnancy supported brain growth. Directives from the family field, your mother's biochemistry, and other epigenetic and genetic factors all significantly shape brain formation.

Stage One: The Reptilian Brain

If your brain started growing normally but, for some reason, stopped growing after twelve weeks, and you were healthy in all other respects when you were born, your life would be very simple. No matter who or what you encountered, you would have only three questions to ask yourself: *Can I eat it? Can I mate with it? Will it eat me?* Your body would respond with a combination of reflexes to suit the answer, and you would behave somewhat like a reptile.

As luck would have it (which may or may not be a disappointment to you), your brain did continue growing after your first three months in the womb, and your reptilian brain was soon joined by your limbic system and neocortex, more sophisticated brain structures. Decision making will never be quite as simple for you as it was for your reptilian ancestors. Always apparent, however, is the undeniable reality that those basic survival instincts are the most fundamental layer on which the human brain is built. *Fight* or *flight*, the two choices animals and humans make in response to stress, are reptilian brain functions.

The reptilian brain, which connects directly to the spinal cord and to the heart,[10] begins developing around day twenty-one or twenty-two after conception. Because it sends messages to what will later be the rest of the brain and the heart, the qualities of the family field during that time will give strong cues for how big the reptilian brain will need to grow to ensure the survival of its owner in the outside world. In short, if your mother and your family are in a fight for survival around the time you are conceived, your reptilian brain will become more dominant than it would if their lives were peaceful at that time. Your reptilian brain picks up cues from chemicals in your mother's blood and signals in your mother's reptilian brain. If she is in a state of relative support and relaxation, with plenty of food, safety, and a permanent home to live in, your reptilian brain will be well trained by the time you are born to act as a stabilizer and supporter to your limbic system and neocortex. It will monitor oxygen levels and regulate sleep and wakefulness, hunger, and sexual urges. If, however, your mother is unsupported, anxious, angry, or unhappy, your reptilian brain will be trained to be on the lookout for predators and will distract your limbic system and cortex into those concerns. Another interesting feature of your reptilian brain is its skill at adaptation. If there is a shortage of nutrients in your mother's diet, you, a developing embryo, even in the first three weeks of gestation, will build strategies to survive the famine you expect to find occurring in your outside world.[11]

You may have noticed in your family or in your friends' families that where previous generations survived a war or a famine, the younger generations who never lived through the circumstances themselves have inherited the hypervigilance required to endure the previous generations' challenges. Behaviors that reflect a fear that money, food, or love will be absent are common objects in the field. The state of readiness your ancestors' reptilian brains were in when they conceived and reared their children gave a cue to the emerging brains of their offspring, signaling them to prepare for more of the same, even if the famine, war, or drought had ended.[12] The environmental forces you were exposed to as an embryo sometimes existed long before your parents were even conceived.

This is why it's essential that, before they conceive a child, prospective parents take time to examine the cues they receive from their own reptilian brains and try to allay or integrate the origin of these significant but obsolete messages before they are passed on to their children. There are ways to enhance the functioning of the reptilian brain so that it does its job of ensuring a baby recognizes she needs food, needs to pull her hand away from a hot stove, or needs to have the urge to run from a herd of elephants charging toward her without also making her hypervigilant about staving off starvation, injury, or death. Parents becoming aware of and healing their hypervigilance will also mitigate what is often a multigenerational and cross-cultural state of reptilian brain "readiness," in which individuals are reared to be on guard for oncoming stressors when there are none.

Imagine that societies have the potential to transform their resonance from violent to peaceful, from on guard to at ease, in the space of one or two generations. Some say it is possible in an even shorter time.

Stage Two: The Limbic System

With the advent of amphibians, a new brain developed that, for the first time, could make more considered decisions about what its owner was sensing. Instead of the simpler reptilian reflexes of eat, be eaten, or mate, the amphibians grew a brain that gave them information about the quality of the food being eaten, the scale of the danger being faced, and the attractiveness of the potential mate. Centers for pleasure, repulsion, and other emotions and sensations arose inside the brain of the amphibian so that it could sense not only what was happening on the outside but what was happening on the inside. Perhaps some radical shift in the earth's atmosphere occurred around this time so that an aptitude for choice suddenly became a tool for survival. Maybe there was enough biodiversity that a higher level of discernment about food, mates, and predators was an advantage.

The limbic system allows a living being to distinguish itself from another living being. If things go well during the second trimester, you will begin to distinguish "me" emotions from "not me" emotions. This lays the foundation for what psychologists call *emotional regulation*: the ability to respond to stress and return to equanimity afterward. If parents can regulate their emotions during pregnancy, their baby learns to do the same.

The family field also gives cues to and shapes the size of the limbic system and its ability to regulate. Genes that prepare the brain to become emotionally ready for a life of survival are turned on when parents or parents' lineages have emerged from and are resonating with survival fields. Genes that prepare the brain for a life of pleasure, comfort, and safety are turned on when parents or parents' lineages have emerged from and are resonating with thriving fields. These developmental habits prevail until the objects in the field and imprints in the parents or baby are integrated.

Imagine the effect the prevailing emotional states caused by war, oppression, hunger, or even workaholism have on the form and function of the reptilian and limbic systems. Then imagine how influential abundance, freedom, good nutrition, and cooperation could be. Because entire generations are often subjected to these objects in the field, differentiating the objects from the identities of the present family and reestablishing supportive, safe conditions before conception can be enough for the developing baby's brain to become emotionally ready to thrive. These steps also make for a happier family, community, and society.

The first two developing systems in the brain, the reptilian brain and the limbic system, form the support basis for the next stage of development, the neocortex. And like the reptilian brain, the limbic system helps regulate the neocortex.

Stage Three: The Neocortex

The neocortex, as it begins its development during the third trimester,[13] introduces architecture that will later support the ability to learn language, think, and stand outside your responses with perspective. Joseph Chilton Pearce, an expert in child development, says that, while the reptilian brain registers present tense only and the limbic system computes both present and past, the neocortex supports the ability to consider past, present, and future.[14] Pearce goes on to describe the neocortex's evolutionary "snag": Awareness of the future also endows the brain with the ability to calculate the infinite number of possible consequences that arise from present decisions. He says this can plague the mind with worry.

Despite the possibility that future awareness may predispose an actively minded person to worry, it also brings a great gift: Future awareness is the attribute from which humans create their dreams. The creative intelligence of imagination wakes out of the neocortex and leads to great possibilities. Solutions to world hunger and poverty, problem solving in the fields of architecture and engineering, and the creation of pathways in computer programming and biotechnology would not have been possible without future awareness.

If the foundations for imagination and the ability to think are laid in the third trimester, consider becoming future aware of what you and all of society can do to support parents so they thrive from preconception throughout pregnancy. After all, a new world is created every time a child is conceived. These new people will grow to be society's builders, teachers, health-care providers, and policy makers. How can you use your imagination to treat babies, even before conception, as sentient beings so that the world they come to expect nurtures their imagination too?

The Triune Brain

The *triune brain* is the combined reptilian brain, limbic system, and neocortex. They are united in this single description because, although anatomically distinct, they are functionally intertwined.[15] The neocortex will only function as well as the systems supporting it. Language, hearing, sight, intellect, and creative ambition—all functions of the neocortex—are regulated and stabilized by the limbic and reptilian systems.[16]

If concerns for survival or emotional well-being are in question at any stage of life, the limbic and reptilian systems are distracted from their job of stabilizing the neocortex, and the neocortex will be lured into scheming survival strategies rather than strategies for creativity. In these situations, by calming and integrating the functions of the limbic system and reptilian brain, the neocortex can often be freed up to perform its "higher functions": a coordination of verbal and intellectual abilities and the pursuit of dreams.

Stage Four: The Prefrontal Cortex and the Orbitofrontal Loop

The *prefrontal cortex* is the area in the very front of the neocortex, right behind the forehead and brow. It makes its debut after birth.[17] Fascinating research is emerging about the prefrontal cortex. This fourth stage of brain development corresponds with the human capacity to experience compassion, empathy, and spirituality. The prefrontal cortex connects the right hemisphere of the neocortex (concerned with creativity and spatiality), the limbic system (concerned with long-term memory and emotional regulation), and the reptilian brain (associated with basic survival functions). Even though the prefrontal cortex does not actually develop until after birth, the environments before then, that is, the three trimesters and the birth itself, profoundly influence how well this advanced brain structure synchronizes with the other structures.

Compared to the estimated hundreds of millions of years that the lower centers have existed, the prefrontal cortex is only about forty thousand years old. The *third eye,* a mystical anatomical structure said to be responsible for intuition and visions, sits front and center in the neocortex, and it is from here that humans contemplate the expanse of time, creation, intuition, and reverence.[18]

The growth of this newest and most sophisticated brain depends, as the other centers do, on experience, so it too is shaped by the environment in which the child is reared. "Its job is to turn the unruly reptilian brain, old mammalian brain, and neocortex into one civilized mind that it may access later."[19]

Toward the end of the first year of life, just before a child begins to walk upright, the orbitofrontal loop develops in the prefrontal cortex. Provided the necessary nurturing occurred during the first year, this loop, which is located right behind the eye, will connect the prefrontal cortex and the limbic system.[20] This means that a well-regulated "stack" of reptilian, limbic, and neocortical patterns will feed back to the emotional limbic system and will develop the basis for well-regulated relationship dynamics and mental capacities. Not surprisingly, it arises at a time when children begin to practice moving away from their parents, discovering their separateness and unique identity.

The Practical Brain

Dan Siegel, MD, has been gathering his own and others' research about the role of the prefrontal cortex. In his book *The Mindful Brain,* Siegel takes three separate fields of research—neuroscience, attachment, and insight meditation—and shows how their findings confirm each other. According to Siegel, neurology attributes the following experiences to the prefrontal cortex:

- Perceiving sensations in the body
- Balancing emotion
- Having insight into ourselves
- Having insight into others
- Experiencing empathy
- Being flexible when plans change
- Modulating fear[21]

Siegel points out that all attachment research (i.e., the study of the effect supportive parenting has on the development of children) shows that the abilities mentioned here are natural outcomes of secure attachment between parents and their children. This means that if children get what they need from preconception through the first three years, they will naturally behave with physical and emotional balance, insight into themselves and others, empathy, flexibility, and the ability to calm themselves when they become afraid.

When Siegel examined the influence of insight meditation techniques, studies confirmed that these techniques served to enhance the same abilities secure parent–child attachment did. As well, two other qualities emerged: morality and compassion.

Another contribution to theories of brain support comes from occupational therapist Bonnie Bainbridge Cohen. In the late 1970s, she stumbled upon a way to help children reorganize their lower brain centers in order to cure their seeming "cortical" or "neocortical" learning disabilities.[22] She called the technique *bodymind centering*. Bainbridge Cohen achieved results no one else could by taking children through movements mimicking reptiles and amphibians. This work showed tremendous insight. Instead of simply training children to speak better or work on their math skills, Bainbridge Cohen understood that revisiting reptilian creeping movements (e.g., moving across the floor on the belly, using the same arm and leg at the same time) or amphibious movements (e.g., pushing off with both feet together or pulling with both hands at the same time) served to integrate and relax the sequencing in the reptilian and limbic brains, reregulating them.[23] Under her tutelage, children and adults found that many of their "higher" brain functions, like verbal and mathematical skills—now stabilized by better-regulated limbic and reptilian systems—were freer to do what they were designed to do. Thinking, creativity, empathy, problem solving, reading, writing, and language skills became easier for those who were previously challenged.

Body-centered practices like mindfulness meditation and bodymind centering are encouraging because they are noninvasive and easy to implement. So even if you or someone you know didn't have an ideal environment as a baby in the womb, at birth, or in the first year, the effects need not be lifelong. Daniel Siegel and Bonnie Bainbridge Cohen, among many others, show us that *the brain is elastic.* (Later in this book, the Intuitive Recovery Project [IRP] offers another opportunity to explore your brain's elasticity and compassionately tend to your imprinting. You can learn what clues to look for in your brain function, body, and behaviors and how to link them to your imprints. Once you have this awareness, you can apply it when you respond to babies, children, and other adults in your community.) First, though, let's look at the influence chemicals have on the developing brain.

The Effects of Chemical and Emotional Fields

You've heard the saying, "You are what you eat." When you are a developing baby in your mother's uterus, this saying holds true. You essentially "eat" what is provided by your mother's bloodstream; her chemicals are yours. Your placenta, which acts as a filter of her blood, is discriminating on your part. It does its best to allow through only what you need to prepare for becoming a person on the outside world. Information received through your mother's blood is one mode of transmission of the family field.

A Caveat

I say the following to the mothers, fathers, grandmothers, grandfathers, and other caregivers reading this book: As you read the rest of this chapter, you may feel that, despite your best efforts, you have somehow hurt your child or children in your care by inadvertently denying your or other children the optimal climate for development. Before you condemn yourself, please consider your concern an opportunity rather than a disappointment. You are part of a society that now supports you with tools to discuss and repair imprints from the prebirth and birth periods. For one of the first times in modern culture, you are free to explore, inquire, and even wrestle with this content. Your curiosity may make the difference between another generation resonating with objects in the field and a generation ending resonance with troubling legacies. Depending on how you take this information, you may be remembered as one of the people who was willing to put into words what was previously unspeakable. You might even consider curiosity as your moral imperative to society, supporting successive generations with your inquiry. It is never too late to heal. And if you are sincerely concerned that you did not do your best, this book can help you take the necessary steps to repair what you missed along the way.

Oxytocin and Cortisol Axes

Let's go back to the brain and the body's chemistry. In his book *Primal Health,* Michel Odent described the *primal adaptive system,* a complex series of chemical and hormonal feedback loops involving the glands, neurochemicals, and immune system products in your body. There are at least thirty-seven million possible enzymatic reactions produced by this series, which is active in every human's body.[24]

When a woman is pregnant, her primal adaptive system has a strong influence on her baby. The mother's hormonal chemistry shapes the baby's developing body much as the stone dropped on the river bottom changed the shape and direction of the river described in Chapter 1. To simplify a very complex system, we can say that mothers share one of two prevailing states with their babies, depending on whether the mother feels like she is thriving or surviving. The internal chemical profile in the thriving state could also be described as an *oxytocin axis,* while the profile in the surviving state is a *cortisol axis.*

What Is the Oxytocin Axis?

In his book *The Scientification of Love,* Michel Odent describes the oxytocin axis by saying, "This is what is going on in your internal chemical profile when you are living in a state of love." Oxytocin is a hormone and a *neurotransmitter,* a chemical that is responsible for transmitting information between cells. It is secreted from the posterior pituitary gland, which sits in the center of the brain, right behind your eyes. Oxytocin is present when you hug, make love, share a meal, breastfeed, or experience general contentment.[25] When babies and mothers are locked in a gaze during breastfeeding or when lovers stare into each other's eyes, oxytocin levels rise.

Being in your mother's womb when she is in this axis will prepare your brain for a world that is relaxed and supported. The oxytocin axis includes the following characteristics, which are explained more fully a little later:

- Blood oxytocin levels increase.
- Blood cortisol levels decrease.
- Muscle tension decreases.
- The limbic system and reptilian brain are well regulated.
- Emotion is peaceful, loving, or even euphoric.
- There is a sense of equanimity and peace.

The life-promoting messages in the oxytocin axis produce ideal circumstances in which to conceive and rear a child. Because the limbic system and reptilian brain are well regulated when you are conceived and grown in an oxytocin axis, you will be free to pursue curiosity and creativity and will enjoy greater adeptness in your coordination after birth and throughout life.[26] Because researchers in epigenetics are discovering that a brain takes growth cues from the chemistry and climate of the mother's environment,[27] development is better supported if a father or trusted companion and the community rally around the mother while she is pregnant; the support of all will raise her oxytocin levels.

Later in life, you seek out experiences that resemble the original axis in which you were conceived and developed. Recall from the section "Recapitulation as a Self-Righting Mechanism" in Chapter 1 the suggestion that your seemingly repetitive patterns, some of which can be self-destructive, may in fact be your being's attempt to repair your original life-threatening messages that may have begun as early as your gestational period. You attempt these repairs in the best way you know how, usually by attracting or recreating environments that will mimic circumstances that caused your imprint.[28] Later, when you read about the IRP, you have the opportunity to learn how to identify patterns in your sequencing that reveal your imprints to you.

Undergoing the intuitive recovery process is not the only way to identify and attempt to repair your imprint. This can occur naturally when you or any person, babies included, is in a slow-paced and supportive atmosphere. There your nervous system naturally reorganizes toward an oxytocin axis, which is the same state as your essential nature, your wholeness. No matter how unregulated the environment you or another has developed from, everyone—babies, children, and adults—knows how to, and will naturally, repair imprints and reregulate their sequencing. Creating an environment that supports an oxytocin axis will encourage your, or anyone's, return to a natural state of balance, even if you think you have never experienced such a state before.

What Is the Cortisol Axis?

In contrast to the oxytocin axis, the cortisol axis describes the state of your internal chemical profile when you are surviving (as opposed to thriving) and living in a state of stress. Cortisol, like oxytocin, is a hormone and is produced in the outer layer (the cortex) of the adrenal glands, small, half-fist-sized organs sitting on top of each of your kidneys.

Cortisol is produced when your body needs more energy to deal with a stressful situation. In response to stress, adrenocorticotropic hormone (ACTH), another neuroendocrine hormone, is sent through the blood from the pituitary gland to the adrenal gland to produce more cortisol. Because cholesterol is needed to build cortisol and to burn fat for extra energy, prolonged states of stress can cause elevated cholesterol levels as well.

At the same time, corticotropin-releasing hormone (CRH), another hormone in your brain that monitors blood pressure and adrenaline levels and stimulates production of ACTH, suppresses your immune system so you can keep moving, uninterrupted by pain, emotion, or illness. In evolutionary terms, being slowed in any way makes prey easier for a predator to catch. When your safety is compromised, your body's intelligence wants to protect you by making you more efficient.

When the stressful situation has passed, and your reptilian brain and limbic system begin to stabilize, your immune system slowly turns back on. How many times have you been struck by a cold as soon as you relax after a demanding stretch of time by going on a holiday or taking time off? This is because your immune system suddenly has a chance to respond, making you more reactive to viruses.

Cortisol is measured by taking a blood sample or a swab of saliva. The amount of cortisol present in the sample indicates how much stress you are under.[29] The cortisol axis includes the following characteristics:

- Blood cortisol levels increase.
- Blood oxytocin levels decrease.
- Cholesterol levels rise.
- Blood pressure increases.
- Muscle tension increases.
- Dehydration increases.
- The limbic system and reptilian brain are in "survival mode."
- Emotional responsiveness decreases.

Although there are many contributors to stress, your body does not differentiate between them. If you are a CEO, an athlete in training, or a person in an abusive relationship, you will have similarly elevated cortisol levels. A baby in the womb cannot differentiate sources of stress; she is only aware that she is receiving life-threatening signals from her mother's cortisol levels. So in a healthy adaptive response, her reptilian and limbic systems grow in a way that ensures they will function best given the cortisol axis/surviving world they anticipate being born into. Babies who grew in a cortisol axis have developed larger reptilian brains that mimic the chemical objects in their family field.[30]

Remember how the worm in Chapter 1's "Expansion and Contraction 2" section contracted in response to life-threatening messages? When mothers, fathers, and communities live their lives marinating in a cortisol axis, the developing babies in that family and community adapt and mimic the behavior and physiology required for survival. Later in life, they will be predisposed and attracted to survival states. In the absence of the survival state, the baby, child, or grown adult will feel uncomfortable and may even create or attract situations that will produce a cortisol axis and an ironic sense of equilibrium. A protective and overactive reptilian brain and unregulated limbic system will prevail, as will immune system suppression and high cholesterol levels.

The cortisol axis imprints and overlays the intact, "ready to grow when the time is right," regulated brain that almost always emerges in supportive, loving environments.[31] With consistent, patient work on the part of parents, caregivers, and/or therapists, the cortisol axis can be shifted and resolved, and this can happen at any age.

Attachment Is the First Addiction

Attachment is a mutual recognition and attraction that develops between a baby and her caregivers, from the earliest hours of life and even before inside the womb. The attachment formed during the hours around birth is of particular interest because of the very high levels of natural addictive substances in both mother and baby. It forms as a result of the reciprocal impression the mother's and baby's chemical, emotional, spiritual, and physical experiences make on one another. This form of attachment is a normal, healthy phenomenon that ensures survival and healthy development of any new being.[32] If all things go well, the baby gets to be close to her mother's skin after birth, and if the delivery has been supported for both mother and child, the oxytocin levels of both will be very high. It may even be that the father or mother's partner, or in the absence of her partner, the birth support people, will experience elevated levels of oxytocin as well, simply from being in proximity to the tender miracle.

Where does addiction enter into it? Alongside oxytocin lingers a powerful group of chemicals called *endorphins*. Endorphins act as strong *addictors,* in that any other chemical present alongside them will become addictive. Nature has designed it this way so that, even though a new mother has worked for many hours in labor, she still has energy and enthusiasm to bond with and care for the child who has just been born. Endorphins, also called *endogenous opiates* because they are made inside the body, dull pain and give mothers a "high." They show up in the bloodstream and can be measured in athletes, lovers, birthing mothers, and babies.[33] Whenever people are excited or in shock, endogenous opiates are present. (There are also *exogenous opiates,* which are created outside the body. These are derivatives of the poppy seed, like opium and its more dilute derivative, heroin. The exogenous opiate Demerol—or Meperidine—is used in hospitals, modeled after nature, and made in a lab but cannot replace the natural endogenous opiates produced by mother and baby's bodies.)

Whatever chemicals are present in the bloodstreams of the mothers and babies—and of the people attending the birth, through field effects—will form significant impressions in the baby's system of what she can expect more of in the future. The chemical, emotional, spiritual, and physical qualities to which she will become attached or addicted can be predicted based on whether the baby has been subjected to a cortisol axis or an oxytocin axis.

The following formulas recap how the axes and addictions work:

- Oxytocin ("love" hormone) + Endorphins (addictors) = Addicted to love/thriving
- Cortisol ("stress" hormone) + Endorphins (addictors) = Addicted to stress/surviving

These formulae, although extremely simplified and perhaps even belittling to those suffering addictions and the complexity of their accompanying experience, can be applied to any endogenous or exogenous chemical (made inside or outside the body, respectively). The requirement for the chemical to become addictive is the presence of opiates.

For example, if *nitrous oxide* (a nervous system depressant that is often used in epidurals and anesthesia) is present at birth when natural opiates are also high, the nitrous oxide will combine with the other existing chemicals and be integrated into a baby's body as "normal." This combination of nitrous oxide and endogenous opiates will become the baseline "norm" against which the baby's body gauges its nervous system regulation. Not only will the baby feel normal later in life only when its nervous system is depressed, but the nervous system will also report itself to be "out of balance" when it is in any other state. Because the first chemical exposures tell a baby what love is, the nitrous oxide will be most closely associated with love, nurturing, and survival. The formula looks like this:

- Cortisol ("stress" hormone) + Nitrous oxide (nervous system depressant) + Endorphins (addictors) = Addicted to stress and nervous system depression

Because the bonds of attachment between babies and caregivers are formed by just about any coupled chemicals, and because early attachment bonds set up "norms" for babies, be aware that babies will tend to recapitulate the circumstances of their prebirth and birth periods throughout their life. Determining the sequencing pattern of birth is one of the more illuminating windows through which to view what an individual is attached or addicted to.

Like many human ironies, attachment as the first addiction has a logical evolutionary explanation. Here is a snapshot of the ideal birth:

You are born. Your mother is warm, awake, and experiencing a profound surge of oxytocin, adrenaline, and endogenous opiates, making her incredibly accessible and deeply eager to hold you, love you, and care for you. Because she is well supported by those around her, she also has the patience to wait for your cue that you are ready for her.

You are slowly beginning to breathe on your own; the first expansion and contraction of your lungs, your first breath! Up until this point, your lungs have had some help draining amniotic fluid (the watery bath you've been marinating in while inside your mother) because you've been deeply massaged by the contractions you and your mother have created together. As you expand and contract your lungs, your bloodstream changes directions inside your heart. A valve in your heart closes for the last time and others open for the first time, and as all these impulses rise and flow within you, and you feel yourself held in the patient expanse of space made available by those who love you. The impulse to reach fires through your body. Now expansion and contraction recruits your whole body. When you are ready, you mobilize yourself from the core of your body and undulate gradually, bobbing your head along the way, up your mother's belly to eventually find her breast, your bare skin on hers, all the while calmly encouraged by her and the others around you. (This sequence, called *self-attachment,* is a continuation of birth.)[34]

This is the second time you will have "birthed yourself" and "asserted your will." The first time was when you traveled gradually down your mother's birth canal. The endorphins present while you self-attach make an indelible imprint that says, "When I go out to make my way in the world, I know the world will support me, just like I feel at this moment." As you grow into a toddler, your caregivers notice that you complete tasks, manage frustration with perseverance, are patient with yourself while you problem solve, and seek out relationships with others who support you as you move, learn, and love at your natural pace.

This is the ideal.

More often, however, things go a different way. A variety of interventions used during labor (usually designed to assist birth processes that have gone awry) can not only interrupt the flow of the birth and the attachment process but also disrupt the presence of the endogenous hormones and chemicals needed to make the flow happen. Although these interventions are often great technological achievements and sometimes life savers, they interrupt the delicate and valuable connections meant to be shared between mother and baby that set the pair up for a thriving life. Cleaning the baby, suctioning fluids out of the baby's nose and mouth, cutting the umbilical cord before baby and mother have stopped sharing blood, pricking baby's heel to take blood for testing, and eye-dropping antibiotics are some routine procedures done even during healthy, normal births and have been known to produce imprints if handled in an insensitive manner.[35] If they are necessary, these interventions are best done at a slow, loving pace while the baby is on the mother's body.

Imagine again that attachment is your first addiction. If you and your mother encounter stress during your first minutes and hours together, your bonds will develop around the feelings, chemicals, and physical, emotional, and spiritual responses you have to them so that later, when you go to bond, you relate through those stressors as though they are your norm.[36]

Sequencing Applied

Now incorporate the theory of sequencing into your prebirth and birth periods. The hour after birth unfolded in a sequence. Birth has a sequence of *stages*. Gestation has a sequence grouped in periods called *trimesters*. The first month of your gestation has a *conception-implantation-discovery* sequence.[37] You may even consider that the way you negotiate coming into your body at conception is a sequence.[38] Each of these sequences, and each aspect of them—the chemical, the emotional, the physical, and the spiritual—is influenced by the family field. They are also directed by a multitude of other unseen forces that are beyond the scope of this book (e.g., the Vedic concept of Karma and/or the concepts of soul and the influence of ancestors).

Although this description suggests that these sequences are separate, none of them truly function independently from the others. They all affect one another, and if we observe how one sequence unfolds into another, we can see how habits in people and societies recapitulate throughout an individual's life and through multiple lifetimes. For the sake of learning and repairing imprints, though, the sequences are approached as separate from one another. You will see why later.

Recapitulation, as discussed earlier, is like replaying a recording that contains the memory of original events, otherwise known as *imprints*. If imprints are not repaired, recapitulation goes on all through life. Even when an imprint is repaired, recapitulation will occur, but you will relate differently because you will have learned to recognize its presence. In Chapter 3, we explore how imprints are recapitulated in musical lyrics, through acts of aggression like violence and war, and in intimacy as individuals love, trust, and show or don't show empathy. But first, let's look at how early, often accidental, animal research showed the importance of the bond between mother and baby as well as the effect interrupting birth has on the ability to produce that bond.

Case Study: Animal Wisdom

Curious individuals throughout modern history who have made a practice of observing the world sometimes accidentally bear witness to intelligent and sentient behaviors, some of which involved how animals relate to one another during the primary period. Long before science and medicine thought to look into the human birth and bonding experience, animals were teaching these accidental researchers that the prebirth and birth periods are impressionable. What made this research possible is that animal births tend to be more public and completely uninhibited. By watching cows, ewes, rats, and even scorpions birth and tend to their young, these scientists were inspired to raise questions no one had ever thought to ask. Although many of the animals observed are evolutionarily distant from humans, and the research was done long before the advent of sophisticated technology and the ability to measure oxytocin and cortisol levels in the blood, these curious observers couldn't help but draw comparisons between humans and other birthing beings.

Eugene Marais was a poet, lawyer, and naturalist living in South Africa from the 1870s until the 1930s. In 1926, while living in the wilderness region of Transvaal, Marais began observing all sorts of animals in their natural habitats, including primates. He published articles about his findings, including "The Soul of the White Ant," which included a section on "Pain and Travail in Nature," otherwise described as "pain and labour."

In the article, Marais described how he had befriended a large, black, female scorpion. After watching her take down a chicken with one sting, he knew to tread lightly near her. One day, he decided to approach her. After lingering some time with her, he found, to both their delights, that she enjoyed it when he scratched her on the back. There was one simple gesture she would perform that indicated to Marais that the scorpion recognized him: When he reached to touch her, she would raise her stinger as though to protect from a foe, but once she got close enough to his skin, she pulled her stinger away and allowed him to continue stroking her.

Later, he observed her giving birth to her young. Watching her in her "travail" and expecting the offspring to emerge as eggs, Marais was shocked to discover sixteen live white scorpion babies emerge from her body. He was stunned by their size and apparent vulnerability. She continued to amaze him with her dutiful and loving treatment of her young. She cut up their food into tiny pieces and fed them carefully, with her stinger raised protectively. It was then that it occurred to Marais that, despite (or perhaps because of) the pain she must have endured during labor, she was extremely bonded with her young. We now recognize Marais's insight as a hallmark of human bonding behavior: that there might be a connection between the pain of labor and love.[39]

After being inspired by his friend the scorpion, Marais conducted his next study, testing sixty Kaffir bucks—a species of sheep from South Africa. Prior to conducting his observations, he had confirmation from farmers that not one single mother had ever rejected her young in the herd during the fifteen years prior to his study. He took six laboring bucks and gave them each enough chloroform and ether to fully anesthetize them during the very last stages of labor. The animals were unconscious for a maximum of twenty-five minutes. He found that all six refused their young after they woke up.

He tried the same experiment with four different sheep, this time using curare, which indigenous peoples use as a paralytic for hunting and warfare. Marais partially paralyzed the four bucks, both consciously and physically, and observed that all four of them were reluctant to receive their young for up to an hour after birth. Eventually, all but one buck took its young. The fourth continued to refuse to bond.[40]

To eliminate the possibility that the animals rejected their young because the anesthetic made them dopey, he repeated the experiments. Instead of giving chloroform or curare at the end of the birthing process, he gave it to the buck right after she delivered her lamb but just before she was able to see her baby. With that last adjustment, none of the mothers rejected their young. Marais concluded that, if the end of labor was interrupted, mother bucks would not bond with their offspring. (Curiously, Marais was an opiate addict. He was known to have a long-standing and unexplained affinity to opium as well as a lifelong addiction to morphine. Perhaps this is not a coincidence.)

Studies illuminating the sensitivity of the bonding period at the end of labor were repeated throughout the twentieth century. Not only did it appear that successful bonding was contingent on an uninterrupted birth, but it was also important not to interrupt mother and baby in the hour following birth. The following studies all show that most species have natural postnatal behaviors that serve to "claim" offspring as their own.

- In 1930, Konrad Lorenz carried out a famous study.[41] He observed that right after ducklings were hatched, their mother's quack served as an orienting device. Lorenz put himself in the midst of a flock of newborn ducklings, imitated the quacking sounds of what would have been their mother, and watched as the ducklings followed him as though he were their mother. They followed Lorenz and his quacking for the rest of their lives.

- In 1956, Helen Blauvelt observed that, if baby goats were separated from their mother before she was able to lick them, the mother had "no behavioural resources to do anything further with the newborn."[42] Blauvelt found this to be true even if the separation was only for a few hours.

- In 1977, Robert Bridges interrupted rats during birth and found the birth was then delayed.[43] Later, he conducted experiments with two groups. In the first, he allowed rats to do a signature form of licking their young right after birth; in the second, he stopped the mothers from spending time with, and licking, their young after birth. He found that if he allowed the mother rats to lick their young right after birth, they could be separated from each other for up to twenty-five days, and when the young were returned, the mother would be completely responsive to them. The mothers who had not been permitted to lick their young after birth were not nearly as responsive to their young as the mothers who had been able to lick their babies.

- Bridges has conducted further studies on maternal memory as recently as 2000.[44] He and colleagues gave rats opiate inhibitors before birth and found that not having access to these "addictors" interfered with their ability to form quick responses to their young after birth.
- In 1979, and again in 1987, scientists conducted similar studies on lambs. The mother and lamb were separated for four hours right after the birth.[45] Half the ewes would not take care of their lambs when they were returned. When left together for a few hours directly after birth, the ewes responded to the lambs even if they were separated afterward.

Animal studies like these, as well as what we know about brain development and the family field model, should make us seriously consider the words of eminent French obstetrician Michel Odent in his book *The Scientification of Love,* where he warns, "We should be wondering about the future of our civilization if the birth process is routinely disturbed in this way."[46]

Questions about Origins

By now, you may have noticed that *The Secret Life of Babies* is introducing a language to help you describe a philosophy that supports the essential nature of all living things and that looks to babies as its emissaries. This philosophy suggests that relationships are deeply imprinted as early as preconception, though imprinting may happen at any time throughout gestation, birth, and the baby's first year of life. If the mother's process of claiming and bonding with her young through postnatal behavior is interrupted, it threatens to eradicate the knowledge of that behavior for future generations and may compromise the survival of the species. Sit with the following questions going forward:

- Where did society first get the idea that pregnancy and birth are medical conditions?
- If society considers the sensations that go with birth to be unnatural or dangerous, how well are humans set to coexist with nature and Mother Earth?

- Given the frequency of birth and gestational sequence interruptions, what expectations about the world might a developing child in the womb or a newborn have?
- Where did science and medicine pick up the cultural tendency to technologize the prebirth and birth periods?

Summary

Over the last eighty years, science has reintroduced the concept that babies of every species are sentient in the womb. This evidence challenges society to consider how it interacts with babies in the womb and during labor and birth.

Brain development as early as the first trimester builds patterns that form the foundation for how children and adults respond to stress and treat others. The reptilian brain begins development in the first trimester and the limbic system in the second trimester. These two regions, which form what is known as the *lower brain,* serve as supports to the later-developing neocortex, which handles "higher" functions of language, ideas, creativity, self-reflection, and compassion, to name a few. The implications are that a mother must be cared for, both during pregnancy and, ideally, before, so that the chemical cues in her bloodstream instruct her baby's developing brain to prepare for a thriving world, one that is eager to receive, support, and encourage.

The emotional, physical, chemical, and spiritual profile of a mother and baby can be described using one of two generalized axes, the *oxytocin axis* or the *cortisol axis,* depending on whether the pair feels they are thriving or surviving, respectively. Depending on their experience in the womb and at birth, babies will form an affinity for one or the other state and will repeatedly seek out similar environments and circumstances—an example of recapitulation.

Animal studies from the late nineteenth and twentieth centuries strongly suggest that interrupting birth with widely used chemical compounds affects the ability of mother animals and their offspring to bond, so much so that offspring survival comes into question.

As you will see in the next chapter, society, present and past, gives near-constant clues to its imprints and objects in the field. By paying close attention to both historical and present-day messages in sequencing and recapitulation, you and all of society can undertake to repair the effects imprints from the primary period have on your life as well as the lives of your family and society.

CHAPTER 3

The Third Principle
Babies Are Our Barometers

Willows never forget how it feels
to be young.

Do you remember where you came from?
Gravel remembers.

Even the upper end of the river
believes in the ocean.
—William Stafford, "Climbing along the River"

The task in this chapter is to consider how today's practices of birth and love, as well as patterns of violence, resonate with events of past history.

Dominance versus Emergence

There is a behavior mode in modern human society that is based, consciously or unconsciously, on a system in which one person's success is predicated on the losses of another. Although survival in nature depends on a relationship of life feasting on death—as does the health of the human body—this social system does not replenish itself as the natural cycles of birth, death, decay, and rebirth do; rather, it tends to deplete resources resisting relationships with each life form in the cycle.

In this section, we explore the roots of what can best be described as *dominance culture.* This is a culture that tends toward individuation as an ideal and avoids incorporating authentic, naturally arising, and spontaneous cues into its values and decision making. Instead, it adopts ideology (as opposed to instinct) as guidance. This "dominance" ethos began to flourish multiple times since the end of the Neolithic period, as migrating and conquering people circled and stretched over much of what is now Europe and Asia. But it reached a nameable cultural crescendo during the fifteenth century in Europe when it became more popularly known as *the Enlightenment.*[1] The dominance culture can be characterized by the loss of relationship (or forgetting of relationship) with the natural world. Due to forgetting that the world holds enough care and abundance for us, humans dreamed up the need for surplus. From there ensued the leaving of the wild for cities and technologies fashioned out of natural resources, and the dwindling of a longtime ceremonial way of taking from the world that Paleolithic and Neolithic peoples were skilled with. The "taking of resources" without first requesting cooperation with gods (who early peoples knew to be these resources) became a norm that has now culminated in a resource-deprived world with economic, agricultural, social, and political crises as the outcomes. For example, genetically modified seeds that produce "stronger" and "more productive" plants, highly technologized processes for childbirth, or disregard for natural capital when assessing the cost of industry characterize a society addicted to a mainly *rational,* individuated, and world-separated approach to life.

Although technology is a culmination of human evolution and genius, its overuse is misguided because it assumes there is something mistaken, wrong, or even irrelevant about nature (which includes weather patterns, plant life, human intuition, and animal intelligence). In a sense, there is a belief that nature is sometimes "right" (usually when it's meeting pleasurable expectations) and often "wrong" (when outcomes are less than desired).

Archaeological findings indicate that, before the dominance culture was established, early seminomadic civilizations revered natural cycles.[2] This was the prevailing cultural ethos from the Paleolithic period (more than thirty thousand years ago) through the early Neolithic period (just over ten thousand years ago).[3] During this time, there was little or no evidence of surprise attack and strong evidence that societies worshipped female deities. Renowned writer Riane Eisler, author of *The Chalice and the Blade* (a monumental work of scholarship on precisely this topic), points out that one of the key qualities of peaceful society was the worship of female deities. This does not necessarily indicate that these early civilizations were dominated by "females"; rather, it suggests that there was a natural intelligence in place at the time that honored the "mother." And who better to revere than Mother Earth, from whom all life emerges? Later, we'll see how cultures that no longer revere Mother Earth are challenged to revere biological phenomena, be they mineral, plant, animal, or human.

It is here that we see a second distinct culture, the *emergent culture.* *Emergent* has a common meaning across such sectors as physics, physical geography, economics, and health care and means organic or naturally self-organized. To get a better sense of *emergent,* think of the synchronization of the flight paths of birds, the organization of schools of fish, the cooperation in colonies of ants and bees, the moon's influence on the tide, the cycle of seasons, and the synchronistic dance of forest ecology. Or consider patterns of fluctuation in the stock market, in organizational behavior, and in embryological development.

All systems, when left to freely interact within themselves and with all their influences, manage to self-organize into recognizable, often cyclical patterns. Emergence itself, which is perceivable across space and time, is in itself not of any shape, size, or time. It does not "live" separated as a thing but, instead, expresses as a consequence of another greater, unimaginable thing. Observing emergence is the closest one can come to perceiving *that* "thing." Revering emergence is accompanied by a simultaneous dissolution of the rational. In the case of humans, lending reverence to the "thing" is not a natural outcome of being born but instead a learned capacity to be in relationship with the greater thing—living plants, animals, humans, and the unseen.

For a long time, dominance culture's rational compass has guided it to success (according to its measure of success) without allowing it to be informed by the natural intelligence—of earth, babies, animals, plants, and so on arising in and around it. Before getting into that conversation further, however, we look at the history of dominance culture and how it may have shaped how nature, animals, and babies are, in some places, still not treated as barometers of the world around them. The next sections examine the cultural inheritances that help maintain today's dominance culture.

Historical Cultural Indicators

Consider domination to be a reaction, an attempt to reclaim power where power has been lost. Consider that power to have been lost as a result of a division. Because no one person, place, or society truly has power yet has imagined that it does and others don't, we should consider power and powerlessness to be a result of some loss, a separation from a whole, and a forgetting of wholeness.

As my teacher Stephen Jenkinson suggested in our personal correspondence between October 2009 and March 2010, "Imagine, if you would, that Europe is not a people, nor is it a place: it is what happened to a people, what happened to a place. It is the reeling away from the unremembered thing." The "forgotten thing" is that Europe is a land whose population (except for the rare exceptions of indigenous peoples: the Basques, Sami, Picts, and others) settled and grew out of the scatter of earlier historical events.[4] The fact that Europe is not a place of original peoples is almost never named, and it may be the most significant reason for its thematic reactions of colonialism, religious elitism, hoarding of the earth's resources, persecution of mysticism, and systematic elimination of intuitive healers and natural medicine.

European Colonialism

Over the course of the last several hundred years, European explorers sought either to expand the empires of their monarchs or to leave the land of their monarchs to find solace from them.[5] Ironically, the term used during this period to describe a colonizing country was *metropole,* a Greek word meaning "mother city."

In the early 1400s, these explorers (many of whom were criminals or adventurers) began charting the seaways to, and eventually drew maps of, the Americas, Africa, Oceania, and Asia. Their relative prowess was measured by the speed with which they captured and resettled these distant lands; in other words, they were ruthless military men, likely having suffered in some way previously at home, who first enticed the indigenous peoples with tools, weapons, horses, and gifts from the distant monarchies and then crushed them through the indirect (though often deliberate) use of disease or more directly through slaughter and rape. In either case, the indigenous peoples were assimilated and forced by their erstwhile "guests" to observe/employ "European" customs, religions, and languages—with catastrophic results for those peoples. Eventually, after roughly blending with the new lands, the European settlers in these new colonies severed the "umbilical lines" to their ancestral "motherlands" by seeking independence from their imperial oppressors: the United States in 1776; South America, beginning with Ecuador, in 1809; and most of Africa by the late 1960s. Canada, perhaps an unwilling toddler, had independence suggested for her in 1867 but did not actually separate from the British monarchy until the 1980s.

What's described here is commonly understood, but what is often missed in discussions of colonialism is that the Europeans also brought their childbirthing and child-rearing practices with them. As a result, indigenous cultures the world over have developed highly interruptive birthing practices.

Europeans as far back as the Dark Ages had begun to see themselves as separate from the earth and the animal world, elements, plants, and wholeness of the universe. (This philosophy of *dualism*, which saw the mind separate from the body/nature/material objects, organized around and was popularized in the seventeenth century by Rene Descartes's philosophy—discussed later in this chapter.) As explorers ventured out into the wilds and perhaps encountered the ungrieved loss of their own indigenous ancestry represented by those inhabiting distant lands, their long-standing dominance culture field prevailed and did not allow them to embrace this part of themselves—in fact, quite the opposite. Dominance culture caused them to destroy the wildness so long forgotten in them. Survival was synonymous with domination of the natural world.

In contrast, indigenous people knew separation from wholeness as a reason to call a healer. Eventually, however, as they were forced to submit to colonial practice, separation became their accepted way of life, with the previous state of wholeness forgotten by or unknown to younger generations. This historical time bears a resemblance to the myth of "Science and Experience" from the Introduction. But where in colonial time did the "great storm" that separated Science from Experience arise? This question takes our exploration deeper into the historical and cultural indicators of religion, philosophy, medicine, and art.

Catholicism

What changes were going on at home in Europe that allowed explorers to treat indigenous peoples as uncultured primitives requiring guidance and lands as expendable resources? As early as the fourteenth century, the Catholic pope issued decrees, known as *bulls*,[6] that "authorized" any and all ambitious adventurers (which Europe was teeming with, due to the dissolution of the original feudal pact between the nobility and the landed gentry who served them) to seize whatever land they could and to "convert" the indigenous peoples to Catholicism, by force if need be. (As of 2013, these papal bulls are still in place, despite requests from legal, governmental, and spiritual organizations to have the Catholic church renounce them.[7])

A combining influence was the Spanish Inquisition, which was reaching a peak at this time. It was not unusual for women to be tortured in response to accusations that they were practicing witchcraft, although most of these women by birthright were healers, midwives, or intuitive in some form of folk medicine. Might the thread that created this general suspicion and persecution of the intuitive art, the female gender, or more fundamentally "The Mother," have been inherited from thousands of years earlier? Could we be looking at an already habituated behavior that at this time had gained enough momentum that it surged over land masses and spread across seas? Why did the political/spiritual authorities authorize these rapacious adventurers to leave the "Motherland" so they could dominate "Mother Earth" in ways that far exceeded any natural urge to explore? What had happened to these men that made them behave this way?

The Enlightenment

During the two hundred years following this willing "separation" of European conquerors and settlers from their Motherlands, and their forced separation of indigenous peoples from their native lands, languages, foods, and customs, European philosophy also underwent a sort of schism. The seventeenth-century French philosopher Rene Descartes, in his celebration of science (in particular mathematics), and in an attempt to free the modern self from traditional and ignorant authorities, chose to differentiate what was, *res cogitans,* or mind and spirit, from *res extensa,* or matter.[8] This made popular the notion that God was the ultimate creator who lives outside space and time and administers creative actions from outside nature and, therefore, outside the body. Deducing from this map, it became popular to think of the body, nature, and all matter as forms of "machinery," guided by and subordinate to the more trustworthy, rational mind. These ideas became the prevailing ethos, and this era eventually became known as the Age of Reason, the Age of Rationalism, or, as mentioned earlier, and without the slightest hint of irony, the Enlightenment.

This theme of separation appears to have had an inheritance about it, much like objects in the field. Through this lens, we can see that it may have been recapitulated from earlier separations, such as the separation of "indigenous Europeans" from their ancestral lands, the separation of healing practices from the intuitive wisdoms of nature-based "folk-medicine," the separation of explorers from their adoptive Motherlands, or the separation of native populations from their reciprocal relationship with nature. This practice peaked with the inevitable conceptual/philosophical separation of the mind from the body. Consider the whole theme of separation to be an imprint in itself.

There is a curious detail to consider along with this. Although the argument suggests that Descartes and, indeed all of "Europe," inherited this habit of separation from earlier events, it is possible that Descartes's dualist worldview may have been a coping mechanism or stress response to an imprint in *his* prebirth and birth period: Descartes was abruptly separated from his mother, who died when he was just one year old. In essence, this entire philosophical shift appears to have grown out of not only previous philosophical and ancestral inheritances, but an early experience he (and how many others?) had actually endured.

Summary

For society to reendow itself with wholeness, it must first understand the epic history it is still recovering from. Great advances have come from a culture that, as the Dalai Lama says, has been "built on individuation." The dominance culture was highly effective at creating wealth for the individual, which is one of its markers of success. However, what has become apparent over the last few thousand years is that success, as defined by the dominance culture, was won at great cost to the family, the village, and the earth.[9]

We are possibly now in an era in which the unsustainability of the dominance ideology is being revealed and recognized. Outward appearances of compliance remain, but more and more people are challenging the polarizing ideologies of the dominant. Its roots are wearing thin, having shot from long distances and antiquated origins.

If we are to cultivate a culture that will thrive sustainably, we must examine society's present-day practices as our words, rhythms, relationship with nature, and relationship to body and disease continue to be profoundly informed, even in the most progressive milieus, by dominance culture values.

In the next section, we explore present-day indicators of dominance culture and look into practices that help palliatively care for that culture as it ages, dies, and possibly reintegrates.

Present-Day Cultural Indicators

The following indicators, with which whole societies act out their prebirth and birth experiences, are becoming so pronounced that, with an attuned lens, you will be able to notice them too.

Language

If imprints have not had the opportunity to come to light, it's unlikely that individuals will explicitly speak of them verbally. However, references to prebirth and birth events are encoded in both body language (e.g., signature movements) and speech (e.g., figures of speech).

Such metaphors as "I'm stuck" (when a project or piece of work is not progressing) or "I feel trapped [in a job or in a relationship]" are common ways to express memories of prebirth and birth challenges. The language is used when present predicaments resemble the circumstances you encountered during your primary period imprint or that caused the object in the field. The figure of speech indicates a place where the imprint or object lives. For example, during a friendly conversation, a man was sharing associations he had made between his birth and qualities he exhibited in his work life. When he was born, his umbilical cord had been wrapped tightly twice around his neck. He was now a successful manager in a large IT company. He said, "I'm able to pop up and do just about anything asked of me." When I pointed out his unusual figure of speech, he, without provocation or any previous training in prebirth and birth psychology, shared the thought that everyone would have preferred him to "pop up" when he was born. He felt his birth had caused his mother, father, and birth staff so much concern that, in order to repay the burden, he could offer to "pop up" to create more ease for his employers.

"I'm in the dark" is another frequently used term that describes the sensation of not knowing what comes next. "I feel like there's not enough air" or "I just need some breathing room" are examples of metaphorical language people use to describe their internal state as they move through a challenging process. Logically, you might wonder why someone needs more air to breathe when there is plenty of space and air around you, or why someone sees darkness in the light.

What causes your or another person's lungs to feel constricted when faced with unknowns or stress? It's almost as though you are encountering a memory in which the space is steadily growing too small, in which oxygen becomes depleted and anxiety rises. At the end of pregnancy, the amount of space and oxygen a baby has becomes limited. This is one of the signals that initiates birth. As well, when unwanted chemicals make their way into the umbilical cord, ultrasound images have shown babies clamping down on the cord to limit the amount of toxic blood entering their body.[10] Babies in the womb can also strategically regulate the amount of toxins they take into their bodies through the umbilical cord by breathing more shallowly.[11] This indicates that shallow breathing is a survival response. In stressful circumstances, all living beings will fall back on coping strategies, some of which they learned in the womb.

"All tied up," being "tied up in chains," "shackled to this ball and chain"—where did these very kinesthetic descriptions come from? Similarly, what are the origins of feelings of claustrophobia in a relationship and the accompanying need to get out? How do they relate to dramatic professions of love like "I can't live without you" or "I just want you, only you!" Are these actually metaphorical retellings of unresolved umbilical cord–placental double-binds or early unrequited love from pre-birth and birth or early infancy experiences? Language is a powerful tool to help locate the source of imprints and is an essential part of supporting children and adults when getting to the source of their struggles.

Song Lyrics

Similarly, when poets, or in this case musical artists, write their lyrics, they sometimes portray feelings through kinesthesia or body language. It is common to have a feeling of resonance with the lyrics of an artist's song even if you don't necessarily understand what is meant by the lyrics themselves.

"Black and White," a song by Sarah McLachlan on her 1997 album *Surfacing,* uses very eloquent prebirth and birth metaphors that describe physical aspects of an intrauterine experience. The lyrics "Unravel me, untie this cord" and "I'm wound up small and tight" might be about an umbilical "cord" and a wish to "unravel" it. The lyrics "On the outside is forgotten" and "everyone is waiting for your entrance, so don't disappoint them" remind me of the many adults I have worked with who, when they regress, recount extreme pressures to "perform" or "get it right" or "not take so long" during their birth. They could feel the expectations of those in the room.

Although these lyrics could very well describe the life of an onstage performer who feels a pressure to shine, it is also possible they have roots in the artist's earliest experiences. The songwriter's lyrics "And I don't know who I am" and "I am the archive of our failure" speak very deeply of a missed experience or some responsibility for a relational breakdown. Her body language is explicit as she pleads for the other to "untie this cord" because she is "small and tight" and "forgotten," fearing that the "center of our union is caving in." The "center of our union" could be where our umbilical cord connects to our navel, the center of our bodies.

Imagining what a baby experiences as she undergoes such intense physical and emotional sensations might provoke you to consider (if you haven't already) just how much babies do feel. If, indeed, adults are recounting prebirth and birth events in their artistic expressions, it might encourage society to recognize that babies must have recorded these memories somewhere, if the artist is now drawing on them later as an adult.[12]

Dave Matthews, another well-known singer/songwriter, could possibly be using prebirth and birth imagery in his lyrics for "Jimi Thing." The songwriter's lyrics "if you could keep me floating, just for a while, 'til I get to the end of this tunnel, Mommy" sound like what a baby might say when asking his mother to continue supporting him in his amniotic fluid or "water" at the end of birth. His request to "Mommy" is compared to the soothing effect when "I take a drink, smoke, sit back and relax, my mind makes me feel better for a short time." Did he come to associate soothing with chemical effects because of a chemical coupling during his birth or nurturing times with his mother? If we could ask the songwriter or his mother about his birth story, I wonder what events would coincide with his lyrics.

Babies, children, and adults, retell their stories in an attempt to convey to others what it was like to experience the event. If the message is understood and provokes an empathetic response, often the imprint from the original event begins to heal.[13] The great secret to decoding all these examples is that people recreate destructive patterns in their lives in an effort to retrieve a piece of themselves that was lost during a challenging early experience or, as mentioned, to have the experience understood by someone else. Without this powerful healing, prebirth and birth imprints and, indeed, any troubling life circumstance can be endlessly recapitulated throughout a lifetime.

The Machine as Mother

It is ten in the morning on Wednesday, and Mary has been in labor since six thirty Monday evening. Her baby is not due to arrive for a few weeks, but she is coming early. Mary was also born prematurely thirty years earlier, but that was a long time ago, and everything turned out fine.

The doctors and midwives have told Mary that her baby's heart rate indicates she is in distress. They need to perform a Cesarean section, and they should do it in the next five to ten minutes. Mary turns to Jeff, her husband, and the midwives. Jeff can see how tired Mary is, and frankly, he is too. He just wants what's best for Mary and the baby. The midwives look at each other, then at Jeff and Mary, and agree that it might be time.

Amy is born fourteen minutes later through an opening in Mary's lower abdominal wall. The doctor cuts through three layers of Mary's abdominal muscles and through the front of her uterus to retrieve the baby. After suctioning Amy's nose and mouth, the birth theatre staff see that she is blue and is not breathing. She is artificially resuscitated en route to the neonatal intensive care unit, where eighteen other babies are in beds near where she will lie for the next three months.

Half an hour later, after Mary has been sewn up, and the placenta that she shared minutes earlier with Amy has been removed. Jeff and the midwives wheel Mary into the neonatal intensive care unit. Amy, meanwhile, has been cleaned, weighed, and placed in a safe, plastic "iso-lette," with a large tube placed in her mouth and taped to her face. She has not yet opened her eyes. Plastic tubes and monitors slowly accumulate in and around Amy. They lie as close to her as she expects her mother to be, the mother she does not yet know she is separate from. The bond begins to form between Amy and the plastic, the tubes, the isolette, and the machines.

Mary is told she cannot touch Amy; the baby is "too premature." The two long to meet on the outside world so they can continue the relation-ship they had on the inside. A window of time in which they could have reestablished and preserved their profound familiarity passes. Mother and baby are not fully estranged, but something sits between them. They think it's them, but it's not. The anesthetic, the separation, the tubing, the lights, and the isolette have informed their bond and, in essence, have come between them. Even though the separation saved their lives, unless these moments, hours, and days are repaired, the memory of the interruptions and their consequences will go unrequited for the rest of their lifetimes.

Massive developments in science and technology let humans survive in a world that might otherwise naturally let us die. Amy's story is an example of the great lifesaving abilities of modern technology, of the support during pregnancy and birth that has arisen as part of the technological progress of culture. With the rise of technology, culture is experiencing an unparal-leled rise in the efficacy of birth interventions. The first Cesarean sections, recorded to have been performed as early as 800 BC, were reserved for postmortem situations—used only after the mother had died.[14] In the 1950s, Cesareans took half an hour;[15] today, a Cesarean can be done in ten to twenty minutes, with fewer apparent risks than ever before.[16]

This faster and safer procedure is cost effective for the medical system and health effective for the mother and baby only in life-or-death situa-tions. But because they decrease time spent in birthing suites, decrease the need for "management" efforts by nurses, and in some cases, are assumed to decrease liability for staff, Cesarean sections are used far more often than needed. Some women experiencing healthy pregnancies have been told, and have come to believe, that pregnancy is a medical condition rather than a life passage. There has been an 80 percent increase in the use of Cesarean sections, and they are used for 80 percent of births in large cities in China, Brazil, and Mexico.[17] Rates of Cesareans in Canada and the United States are, on average, 30 to 40 percent, even though research from the World Health Organization indicates that a country's Cesarean rate should not be more than 15 percent.[18]

Since it is already known that a baby born with anesthesia in her system will have a slower response to bonding that, if not repaired, might affect her emotional and physical development,[19] it might be our cultural imperative to include the mother's and baby's well-being as an important marker of birth intervention success.

This is not to criticize the doctors, nurses, midwives, and other medical staff involved in birth interventions. In neonatal intensive care units, babies born as early as twenty-five weeks (and in some cases, even surviving at twenty-four weeks) are being nurtured with great skill, patience, and insight until their lungs and digestive systems have matured enough for them to breathe and feed on their own. The people who do this should be acknowledged and applauded. But because the early stages of life are designed for babies to learn rapidly about the world around them, we need to be aware that they can be imprinted with the sounds and rhythms of machines—heart monitors, blood pressure gauges—and the look and feel of the incubator. They are clever to orient to the machines around them. Their life depends on bonding with their mother, and in her absence, they will bond with whatever is closest to them, anything warm and making sounds.[20] This might be mother and father, same-sex parents, adoptive parents, siblings, friends. and in some cases, inanimate objects like toys or machine. A baby's point of reference for the world is, by definition, made by the collective imprint of her experience from preconception through conception, gestation, birth, and the minutes, hours, days, and weeks after birth.[21] So it is important to accompany lifesaving measures with reparative measures.

In the next chapter, we look at ways to bring human connection and sentience to the technologized birth so that even babies who have gone through life-threatening situations, despite the presence of stress hormones, machines, bright lights, possible rough handling, water, needles, and suctioning sounds, will experience, above all, positive, life-promoting messages from their mother (because she is made to feel comfortable and safe), patience and support from birth supporters, and compassion for the initiation they are passing through.

One commentator has noted, "The kids of the next generation are being born with technology in their hand; it is no longer separate from them, but an appendage."[22] Is technology at birth and in early infancy replacing flesh with plastic, their mother's and father's voices with the sounds of machines and lights, and human smells with synthetic and sterile ones? And if this is the case, can hospitals and caregivers include as much human touch and sound as possible along with the technological support so the mother, and later the friend or lover, is not replaced by a machine?[23] Studies support the idea of giving babies as much skin contact with their mothers as possible, even if they are premature.[24] And although culture is indebted to the genius of technology and its life-supporting capabilities, it is every person's obligation to recognize the deep impression technology makes on babies, mothers, and our culture as a whole and to differentiate its influence from essential nature. Caregivers can ensure that babies are held skin to skin, talked to, and allowed to hear the voices of and smell the odors of their mothers and other family members alongside any technological intervention during birth and early infancy.

Suicide and Drug Abuse

Although the discussions of language and technology have introduced some compelling ideas about memories of early events, this section contains some harrowing and conclusive evidence that early experiences are remembered and recapitulated.

A correlation has been found between suicidal behaviors and the events surrounding birth. The World Health Organization became interested in how many people committed suicide the world over. They looked at the statistics in developing nations and published the following figures, which represent the number of fifteen- to twenty-year-olds per one hundred thousand people who committed suicide in each country:[25]

- Switzerland: 14.9
- Austria: 13.8
- Hungary: 12.3
- Ireland: 11.8
- Czech Republic: 10.3
- Poland: 9.6
- France: 9.1
- Sweden: 8.3
- Germany: 8.0
- Denmark: 7.8
- UK: 7.3
- Holland: 6.4

Although attempts have been made to explain the reason for higher suicide rates in some countries (e.g., people in countries situated between the forty-fifth and sixtieth parallels spend a greater number of hours in darkness during the winter and experience, on average, colder temperatures), some findings do not correlate with latitude predictors at all. In fact, it appears that certain countries' suicide rates are correlated with their birthing practices.

For example, the country listed here with the lowest rate of youth suicide is Holland, which is unique where childbirth is concerned. In this country, 82 percent of midwives work independently from the medical system. When a Dutch woman discovers she is pregnant, she most often visits a midwife. The midwife will decide, during pregnancy and labor, if the advice of a doctor is needed. The effect of this system is that about 30 percent of births occur at home, and many hospital births are attended by a midwife, who does not answer to a doctor. The rate of Cesarean sections is around 10 percent, and the rate of epidural anesthesia remains less than 10 percent. When you add that, among this group of European countries, Holland also has the lowest overall rate of suicide, it becomes suggestive.[26]

These European statistics might inspire other comments. For example, the rate of youth suicides is higher in France, even though part of the population lives below the forty-fifth parallel, than it is in Sweden, where a part of the population lives above the sixtieth parallel. The rates of obstetrical intervention are also much higher in France than in Sweden. Similarly, the rate of youth suicides is higher in Ireland, where labor is more often "actively managed" than it is in the UK.[27]

Compare statistics from North America for the same age group and approximate time period:

- Canada: 11.8 per 100,000[28]
- USA: 9.9 per 100,000[29]

Swedish researcher Bertil Jacobsen, MD, conducted a series of studies that looked at the issues facing present-day drug addicts and people who had committed suicide after 1940. One study looked at amphetamine addicts. It was shocking to discover that a correlation existed between the number of mothers given nitrous oxide (an anesthetic) during labor and their babies' addictive tendencies in adulthood.[30] In another study involving two hundred men and women addicted to opiates (heroin or an opium derivative), a correlation was found between addiction and mothers being given opiates, barbiturates, and/or nitrous oxide during labor.[31] To ensure that it was, in fact, their birth environment that was at the root of these people's addictions, Jacobsen did another study in which he ruled out the possibility that other factors, such as socioeconomic status and being raised in neighborhoods with a high number of drug users, had anything to do with addiction. The results of the new study still showed that drug addiction seemed to be connected to being born in hospitals with birthing practices that included administering drugs to birthing mothers.[32]

Jacobsen then took the studies a step further and looked at possible connections between suicide and injury at birth. The results were harrowing:

- Suicide victims who killed themselves by asphyxiation had been asphyxiated at birth.
- Suicide victims who killed themselves by violent means had suffered mechanical trauma at birth.
- Suicide victims who killed themselves by taking drugs or poison were born under the influence of pain-managing drugs.[33]

Some of these studies were repeated in other countries during different years and were found to have the same results.[34] Similarly, researchers who studied the birth data of violent criminal offenders found that babies subjected to a painful birth intervention and separation from their mothers after birth were more likely to commit violent criminal acts later in life.[35]

The concern when first reading these results is that mothers may feel guilty that they used pain relief to help them give birth or that families who required the use of forceps to deliver their child will expect their children to become drug addicts and suicide victims. Please don't jump to these assumptions! It is inaccurate to suggest that birth interventions always lead to suicide and drug abuse. Rather, they are one of many conspiring contributors to a life of discomfort. Jacobsen's studies highlight the value of supplying those suffering from addiction and suicidal tendencies with the support of practitioners trained to correctly identify recapitulations and help repair the imprints associated with them. In this way, early challenging experiences can be treated and present-day grievances eased. These studies are also motivation to reconsider the long-term effects birth interventions have on the health of a society and to do our best to reduce or mitigate their use.

These Swedish studies and others like them are important to policy makers because they provide a scientific correlation between events at birth and later health challenges. Going back to what we learned in Chapter 2 about "attachment being the first addiction," it follows that, when a nervous system depressant makes its imprint on a newborn baby, the baby may grow to become an adult who seeks nervous system depressants. Mechanical pressure imprinted at birth may compel a person to seek states that mimic that pressure later in life. How may emotional and chemical tendencies have prebirth and birth experiences at their roots?

If, as the studies suggest, an individual will seek out a medicated or painful existence if such a state is established as the "norm" at birth, this maintenance can be a near full-time pursuit for a person and a significant burden on the economy and health care system. Why, then, since all the studies mentioned satisfy scientific scrutiny and are considered to be of the same caliber as those used to justify the use of medications and the implementation of health policies, is the connection between prebirth and birth experiences and problems in later life not on the cultural conversation plate? Why has the wisdom they have exposed not been absorbed by the medical world with radical changes to birth practices and a decrease in unnecessary birth interventions? After all, if society recognizes and is compassionate to babies with Fetal Alcohol Syndrome and drug addictions, why does it not recognize the danger of medications and other interventions during pregnancy and birth? Is it because the results are more immediately visible with fetal alcohol? Or is it easier to accept alcohol's consequences on the baby because it was delivered by the mother rather than by the hospital staff? If we believe alcohol, cigarettes, and recreational drugs have lasting effects on the neuroimmune systems of children and adults, why don't we extend that belief to include chemicals prescribed during pregnancy and birth?

With the incidence of mechanical and chemical imprinting that is going on today in hospitals around the world, what qualities and challenges will the new generation be facing? And finally, is society as in the dark as it appears to be when it comes to the origins of self-destructive behaviors? Or does it at times choose to shrink back into silence at the possibilities of its own contributions?

Case Study: David

David, a husband and father of two, was adopted the moment he was born. Although he suffered the deep loss of his birth parents that day, he was taken into a loving home and raised alongside two other siblings. David was reintroduced to his birth mother when was in his thirties. Several years later, she told David that there was yet another painful event in their short history together: When she was two months pregnant with him, she had taken pills in an attempt to abort him.

The day I sat down with intelligent, pleasant, and engaging David, I noticed his eyes darted from here to there. His train of thought shifted just as quickly, as did his body language, as if both were saying, "I can't stop moving, and I'm going in all these directions at once."

In conversation, he rapidly jumped from information about his recent seizure, to details of having had a sore back, and then on to his use of muscle relaxants and painkillers.

In the midst of his seemingly disconnected yet vitally important pieces of information, I had to interrupt him. "So David, what do you feel is going on?"

David's eyes flitted briefly to mine, and he said, "I can't seem to get off the painkillers. My back pain is gone, but I'm using the drugs . . . all the time. I'm hiding them from my wife."

Right away I thought of his birth mother's abortion attempt. "David, I'm remembering what you told me about your birth mother and her taking the pills."

He said, "Yeah, I know, I guess that's a big deal. But does it really matter? I'm here now, aren't I? I'm fine now. Guess I'm really strong, hey? I've always been strong."

I said, "Yeah, David. You *are* strong. You're so strong. But did you ever consider that maybe you had to be strong to survive what you went through? I wonder if you ever considered that maybe your affinity for drugs isn't because of you. But perhaps you had to incorporate them into your bloodstream as though they were part of you in order to survive?"

For the first time since he had sat down, David focused his eyes directly at me. His gesticulations stopped, and his speech became coherent. David had always known his early experiences were tough, but their impact on him had remained secret to him. Now that impact was being revealed. He had heard the stories, but until that moment, he hadn't connected the details to his current suffering. And despite their sad and upsetting reality, something about the words I had uttered—"this may not be because of you"—freed him. Even though David wasn't suicidal, he could have easily been called self-destructive.

Soon after our meeting, David entered rehab. When I spoke to him a month later, he said, "You know, it's been so many years since I could feel anything. I had no emotions. It's been many things that have helped me get back to myself, but perspective has given me my emotions again."

And he had an insight for us all. "This . . . it doesn't discriminate. Whether you're homeless or a Supreme Court judge, it can get ya." He was talking about drug addiction. And I was thinking about how many other drug addicts had had drugs in their system during their prebirth and birth periods.

War

We have discussed how the birth environment creates a reference point to which individuals attempt to return throughout life, but what about other qualities of the early environment? If an entire society has endured a circumstance together, like war, do predictable patterns emerge in the culture itself as well?[36]

In his keynote address to the Association for Pre- and Perinatal Psychology and Health, psycho-historian Lloyd De Mause noted the following patterns about nations at war. After collecting historical material from magazine covers and political cartoons, he noticed that war was most often depicted using metaphorical prebirth and birth language.[37] For example, terrifying, bloodthirsty women were depicted presiding over war (rather than being the victims of it, which is more often the case) all through later antiquity and into the modern day. Even Saddam Hussein's description of the Gulf War had prebirth and birth overtones. It was to be "the mother of all wars." Political cartoons during that time showed women hovering over the battlefield and ordering soldiers into battle.

The consciousness of countries preceding wars seems to hold a collective fantasy of a female enemy who is sexually voracious and murderous. For example, prior to the French Revolution, the belief that the queen, Marie Antoinette, was "a vampire who sucks the blood of the French," eventually led to her execution by guillotine.[38]

De Mause described other media phenomena in the lead-up to wars, citing movies like *All about Eve* before the Korean War and *Cleopatra* before the Vietnam War. The Persian Gulf War was preceded by a trend of femme fatale movies such as *Fatal Attraction* and *Thelma and Louise* as well as the popular television series *Dangerous Women*. De Mause suggests that these films represent a prevailing collective memory in countries (particularly America) prior to war of the power-wielding female. He theorizes that this memory is born of imprints from less-than-desirable beginnings in the womb.

Interestingly, he goes on to show that, after war breaks out, and the tensions building between nations become explicit, the dangerous female is then freely objectified onto the enemy. Saddam Hussein was depicted in cartoons as a "dangerous pregnant mommy" with a nuclear bomb in his womb and also as a mother holding a dead skeletal baby.[39] Before the War of Independence from England, Americans felt "poisoned by Mother England."[40] During the McCarthy Era in the United States, it was proposed that the "national life-blood was poisoned" by Communists.[41] Is it not curious that countries fighting for safety and independence use metaphors of a struggle with mother, pregnancy, blood, and a poisoned bloodstream?

According to De Mause, objectifying the mother—and females in general—as an enemy dates back to antiquity, when wars were "imagined to have been fought against often powerful and frightening females."[42] These women were often the mothers of the hero god—for example, Tiamat and Ishtar of Babylonian mythology and Kali from the Hindu tradition, to name a few.

De Mause and others speculate that entire nations play out traumatic imprints from the primary period. If birth, pregnancy, and even conception have been "poisoned" by toxic, painful, or untrustworthy circumstances, children, adults, and then collective nations will take on habits reflecting the early circumstances. Because the imprinting is expressed in the preverbal language of the not-yet-born or newly born child, styles of blame and attitudes about victimhood come to be expressed as cultural habits. Once a generation of people has been born through toxic or repressive experiences (e.g., the use of ether and chloroform for anesthesia in the late nineteenth and early twentieth century, spinal blocks through the mid-twentieth century, twilight sleep during the 1950s and 1960s, and forceps and Cesareans in the last fifty years), they are likely, as a culture, to regard sedation, numbness, and pain or violence as normal as well as something to rally around. Mistrust will extend to those who touch, love, or gain the trust of people and cultures born through these betrayals. The natural sense of accomplishment a baby achieves as she works through birth together and in cooperation with her mother is an ideal, but if this sense of accomplishment is never discovered, it will be replaced by more violent and aggressive attempts to achieve independence, either as an individual or as a nation, while "saving and purifying" the "Motherland," ridding her of all pollutants.

If cultures under pressure are reminded of the tastes of poison, violence, and betrayal, and the data supports the idea that babies remember their earliest experiences, then is society not obligated to look at the very earliest experiences of its members in order to encourage the global peace it so wishes to see in the world? If governments are interested, health practitioners can be trained to prevent prebirth and birth imprinting on the new generation, and citizens and practitioners can be trained to help resolve the effects imprints have already made on previous generations. If the numbers and logic are there, what holds society and its policy makers back?

Summary

Knowing that prebirth and birth imprints are encoded, and identifiable within cultures in language, song lyrics, addictions to technology, drug use, and patterns of violence like suicide and war, members of society are called to action that uproots the status quo.

If children are routinely birthed into technological environments and separated from the live bodies of their mothers for reasons of necessary medical interventions, will they then seek out those relationships with technology, medications, and physically painful circumstances as though they are normal? In highly technologized births, are we not informing the bond with first love—the mother—with myriad contradictory stimuli? Is there a correlation between the most difficult early moments and society's exponential assimilation to self-destructive behaviors? And how much creative, life-sustaining energy is unconsciously rerouted in an attempt to repair the early experience? What if citizens of the world were protected from unnecessary pain and nervous system–altering medications and instead supported by skilled practitioners who could deal naturally with the common and natural impasses of birth? When it is determined that a birth intervention such as anesthetics, forceps, or a Cesarean is necessary from a life-or-death perspective, what if we then routinely offer prebirth and birth therapy to those mothers and babies so they can recover? What if every community across present-day culture possessed the tools and the trained individuals to prevent and repair imprints to and from this delicate period? Where then could human energy flow instead? How much energy could be freed to pursue self-actualization and life-sustaining behaviors that are presently relegated to conceal and inadvertently mystify the roots of suffering?

PART TWO
Experience

CHAPTER 4

The Fourth Principle
It Is Never Too Late to Heal

Trust yourself, then you will know how to live.

—Johann Wolfgang von Goethe, *Faust*

The Vision Horizon

Dominance culture (introduced in Chapter 3) is defined as a society that takes its directives largely from the logical and ideological. It tends to dominate or dismiss nature, human emotion and intuition, and intelligence arising from babies, children, animals, and other living things. Dominance culture has served itself well, and although it endows present culture with genius, it has unknowingly, and sometimes knowingly, cut a destructive swath through much of humanity to do so.

Although the dominance culture has been reinherited and recapitulated for the last six or seven thousand years, there are signs that the planet's societies are shifting away from the dominance habit. A trend, one that has moved in and out of focus over millennia, is building its presence. As you look around, you might see evidence of the spontaneous change, transformation, reunification, or reemergence of *emergent culture*.

Disbanding Dominance

Disbanding the dominance culture does not require persuasion, force, or rejection of its principles. In fact, any hostility toward the dying system will, ironically, sustain it, because hostility is a relic of the very separation that gave birth to it. As dominance slowly retires and a new way evolves into being, society might resist its habit to respond to duress with divisive reactions by labeling outdated social structures as "less than." Because dominance culture is an inheritance, a recapitulation of myriad ungrieved losses over centuries, its only salve is cross-cultural grief and compassion. If you have experienced any amount of grief and tenderness toward losses of your own, then you might wish to turn these same sentiments toward the dominance culture. It too suffers and has greatly. Compassion, a type of "medicine," if you will, is essential.

Emergent Culture

We had a brief introduction to emergent culture in Chapter 3. It's up for discussion whether this is a new culture dawning or vestiges of predominance culture that have been preserved and are blooming again. Although much valuable scholarly work has examined how cultures rise and fall, this section is not meant to summarize this research and determine the exact alchemical routes that have led to today's hybrid world; rather, it attempts to describe a cultural style that, although an outgrowth of all that has preceded it, is founded on conscious relationship with all things living. Emergent culture, rather than having central tenets that would make it dogmatic, can be identified by the activities and sentiments around which its members organize their lives.

So how does this self-organization, or emergence, look in a culture? Emergent cultures perceive, interpret, and revere life with the awareness that how they do so is integral to life living itself. In other words, the quality of the culture's responsiveness makes it possible for life itself to thrive. Tree does not stand alone and sing to herself, nor does tide move for her own sake. We take pleasure, shelter, cleansing, and food from the living things around us. What do we do to earn these daily gifts? Nothing. But, our awe and the offerings we can't help but make (gasps, songs, paintings, dances, poetry, and the like) in response to them may be the very "food" they require in order to live. Our willingness to sing back—essentially to be moved—is our side of what could be a call and response. The perceptive skills humans are endowed with can allow them to adopt directives from nature for decision making. Emergent culture is a society who does not see itself as a "steward" of the planet, or a savior, but as Mexican doctor and healer Miguel Ruiz says, as "one of the organs of the earth."[1] In other words, rather than humans calling themselves "the problem" for why the atmosphere and our systems have fallen out of balance, and are therefore in need of a "solution," they can instead redeem the health of the planet by perceiving, interpreting, and revering her. This is something we'll look at soon in the Intuitive Recovery Project (IRP). Tens of millions of people around the world already embrace this culture, and some, including many indigenous peoples, never stopped embracing it. Some emergent societal practices that have integrated into modern culture include the following:

- biodynamic farming, which is the practice of seeding, growing, and harvesting crops in coordination with the moon and planets' positions
- the ancient medical practice of Ayurveda, which uses a sophisticated and holistic paradigm to treat human, relational, and environmental health
- horse and dog whispering, in which people attuned to animals help other humans achieve harmony with these creatures

All are examples of whole-system lenses with humans perceiving from inside the system rather than as unrelated overseers peering in.

Emergent culture is the remarriage of Science and Experience, with Knowledge, which can only arise from the unity of the two, resting at that place where sentience intersects. It suggests that our understanding of our way and place in this world arises through reciprocal relationship with nature.

Emergent Ecology

Wikipedia defines *ecology* as "the study of organisms and their environ-ment," and *human ecology* as "the relationship between human groups and physical and social environments." Moving from the definition of emergent culture, I would define *emergent ecology* as the study of humans participating with the physical and social environment, or rather the study of all living and unseen creating environment.

Ecology and economics are two of the major topics on the cultural conversation plate, for obvious reasons. Peak oil, global warming, rising sea levels, and an increasing number of natural disasters all provide com-pelling motivation for consumer society to shift its habits. Some even say it is too late, that if the world's societies stopped their consumption of fossil fuels today, there would be no chance to reverse the damage as the mean temperature of oceans and corresponding changes in salinity would not support a sustainable Earth atmosphere.[2]

Secondary to economy and environment are widespread poverty, hun-ger, disease, and violence, which many of the world's most influential people never see firsthand—or some might say, which they are more adept at ignoring.

The driving concerns about all these issues are fear (that things need to change or we will die) and morality (or more aptly, guilt). We have, however, already learned what happens to your brain in a cortisol axis: When you are in a state of stress driven by fear or guilt, this axis shapes your decisions.

So could sensory recovery be a first step in an authentic, non-fear-driven, non-guilt-driven path that will make the world more habitable for everyone, not only a precious few? Could following our senses and using them as skills to perceive, interpret, and revere life achieve change through an oxytocin axis?

Emergent ecology introduces a new angle to the initiative. It does not exclude the gravity of difficult realities, but it does not let them lead the decision making. Instead of trying to motivate the world's population to care about the planet out of guilt—or instead of scaring the world's population into action on behalf of ecology—return the human to a vessel of love. If you and everyone around you knew you intrinsically mattered to the success of everything and that everything around you considered you, felt you, moved in concert with you, what decisions would you make then? This is emergent culture's contribution to the ecological movement. It reframes the world's issues through this lens: If every being knows he or she matters, then he or she will treat everything as though it matters too. No one will have to force another to care about something if they already care about themselves.

So how do we start knowing we matter? We may be a generation out, but by reimaging village behavior (no small task, and worthy of another book in itself), which includes restored rites of passage, we can ensure that babies are prepared for and welcomed before they are conceived. Children who come into the world knowing that they matter treat everything else with equal matter too.

An emergent ecological practice can't help but restore your intimacy with those things that you might think are living "out there," away from you. The rains, the birds, the earth, the winds, the islands, and the landmasses are not independent and neither are we. It's also fair to say that emergent ecology is redundant. Without environment, there is no human, and vice versa. Vietnamese monk Thich Nhat Hanh refers to this recovery from dominance culture when he says, "'I think, therefore I am' really means 'I think, therefore I am not.'" He says that the kingdom of God is in the flower, in the body, in the earth, and in every manifestation. Emergent ecology, then, is more of a practice than a study. It means a way of life that begins with recovering sensory skills and leads to the capacity to participate in verbal, tactile, and psychic relationships with the flower, the body, the earth, and in every manifestation, seen and unseen.

Preparing the Way

So the path from dominance culture to emergent culture contains a set of practices and activities that naturally stimulate relationships. Through relationships, the shift may appear small-scale, its platform in the personal, the familial, and the communal. But this smallness is deceiving. As soon as relational gestures are initiated, the field shifts too, naturally bringing other living systems with it. Because of this, global transformation need not to be a goal. Whole system and whole planet coherence is rather implied and embedded in each being's relational gesture and in the response from who they gesture toward. The following sections describe some habits that will influence how the conversation continues.

Emergent Language

Contained in words are not only sounds, syllables, and—when they are transcribed—letters but also emanations from thoughts, feelings, and senses. For this reason, any society's words are potent reflections of what it senses and, in the case of etymology, the history that led to their meanings. How often do you find yourself using the following terms to describe how you feel about a situation: right/wrong, good/bad, normal/abnormal, or sick/healthy? What if terms could extend further than categorizations or polarized judgments? What if "bad" was only a starting point for what "bad" feels like at that given moment for the person using it? Why stop at "bad"? Where is "bad"? What do you know about "bad"? Does it have a color? A texture?

When you become curious about what "bad" feels like, how "right" appears, and where "normal" is derived from, you invite language to come alive and become a vehicle with which you can elaborate your internal experiences and share them with others. If you share an experience with a friend, the two of you will have different words for your internal experiences, but both can be heard and understood, even if told differently. What freedom might you find if words can include descriptions of your sensual experience rather than simply the preprioritized category your experience fits into? How can words enhance your capacity to praise nature, sunrises, storms, your body and its sensations, and your emotions? If you cease to fit yourself and your experiences into a "norm," it will be possible for your experiences, and those of everyone else, to transcend "right" or "wrong" and become living, dynamic scenes.

What if language first arose from a sequence of spontaneous sounds that living provoked from inside the human body and that had their origins in nature? Try exploring and experimenting with the question: From where do I collect my senses every day, and how closely do my words reflect what I sense?

A Reverence for Nature

Emergent culture and sustainable living rest in the ability to sense and know (in a body-centered way) that which is being sensed and to respond to what is sensed. In short, you come into a deeper relationship with your senses and, therefore, the world around you. David Abram, in his book *The Spell of the Sensuous,* describes sensing as multidirectional: You are sensed as much as you are sensing. He speaks of reaching to the plant, knowing the plant is equally reaching to you. He talks of the "membrane of the world," which includes all living things, and writes that the membranes of our bodies are continuous with those of other living beings.[3]

And so the wind is brushing up against you just as you are brushed by it. The contact between any two forces and the registering of that contact deep within each system creates the next step of life. The wind will shift around you and grace its next surface while your skin will pucker and enliven, causing you to respond with your next step, whether it's to take shelter, become delighted and wish for more exposure, close a window, chant a prayer of recognition of the elements, or any exponential number of other possibilities. What would it be like to wonder aloud what it might have taken for the wind to have arrived at your door? To have seen what it has seen? Much of this happens naturally without your registering what you sense. But for a moment, consider how many moments of relationship to what is sensed slip past your and others' awareness. Could you really take in every thread of stimulus in a day? Would you survive, or might you become overstimulated?

First Peoples developed ways to live in harsh weather conditions long before the advent of modern technologies. Some of them continue to possess the skills to do so today. Many, however, including the portion of the population disconnected from their aboriginal ways as a result of repeated migrations and missionizations, would not survive the outdoor climate without employing dominance culture adaptations to weather. In fact, most of the world, save a small handful of indigenous tribes, chooses to enjoy the benefits of technology. The temperatures of homes and offices are controlled by machines or computers; clothes are cleaned and dried by machines; foods are cooked in electrical, gas, or microwave ovens; and clothing is made in a lab to be weather resistant. In some cities in North America, walkways and underground parking allow the luxury of surviving the winter without having to step outside. Life spans have transformed because of these technologies, and indeed, they are quite pleasurable, but they also mean that business continues at any hour of the day, in any season; rhythms are organized around productivity; and human self-regulatory interruptions are kept to a minimum.

Given this reality, is society able to sense the natural world and still carry on in a modern and productive way? Would it even want to? What is the emergent approach? Perhaps it is a blend of benefitting from exposure to nature and enjoying the benefits and comfort of technology. Perhaps the question is not how to choose one over the other—technology over nature or vice versa—but how we can use words to praise the materials or machines we use in order to show their elements that we know where they have come from. What would it be like to reanimate the very materials around us with our speaking of them?

One limiting factor in the use of technology is speed. Technology quickens transmissions to a rate faster than humans are able to integrate them. We register their message, but there is not a deep sensing. Why is it that text messaging has become illegal while driving? It's not only because looking away from the road is dangerous, but also because becoming emotionally or intellectually (or sensually) involved in something other than the immediate surroundings can be lethal when operating a large piece of machinery like a car. Could it be lethal for the human body even when large machines are not involved? Could it be lethal to fall out of relationship with the world? And for whom is it lethal? Human senses have not yet evolved to where they can be used at the speed of present-day rates of stimuli and still respond as though they're intrinsic to the whole ecosystem rather than separate from it.

In the article "Green Nature and Human Evolution," plant biologist Charles Lewis describes how animals in the forest can sense oncoming rains and will take shelter long before the storm arrives. He attributes their predictive behavior to rapid changes in barometric pressure, a phenomenon known to cause migraines and regular headaches and to exacerbate arthritis symptoms in humans. Lewis points out the connection to humans and suggests that human headaches and arthritic worsening are evolutionary "leftovers" from our primate ancestors, an "intelligence" in our bodies that signals us to take cover should we hope for the best survival outcomes.[4] In a culture that has its intellect and reason dominating its senses and responses to nature's cycles, weather could be perceived as inconvenient and as an interference with productivity. In this context, the symptoms arising from a change in barometric pressure are best handled by taking a pain medication and eventually seeking a diagnosis to understand the difficulty.

Emergent culture invites you to embrace the gifts offered by dominance culture technologies while still resourcing authentic responses to what is sensed and spending more time with nature in order to learn from her—taking trees, animals, plants, and even babies as teachers. In an emergent approach, before you interrupt your sensation—be it pain, hunger, emotion, or the sense of an oncoming storm—consider welcoming what is sensed to fully enter your awareness. Then explore your authentic response; see whether it is to slow down, take cover, rest, eat, sleep, call someone who comes to mind, or something else.

Emergent Body

Every atom and every cell moves. Without movement, there is death. Even though the form of your body appears solid, every space, even the ones in between each of your cells, is moving. How did the first cell learn to move? What taught it to move? What was the first movement?

Remember back to Chapter 1, where you read about stillness and expansion and contraction. Imagine your rhythms, both inside your body's cells and in your daily routines. Consider what it would be like if your life, your work, your social life, and your parenting were designed around your natural sleep and wake cycles and the most digestible times to eat. Imagine if your activities were shaped around natural quiet, creative, active, and restful periods, essentially around trusting your natural body movements. How would a set of three days look?

If you were given the opportunity, would you be able to differentiate your authentic rhythms from those the dominance culture is built around, with a work schedule beginning in the morning and lasting until dinner? This routine is widely accepted in North America and most of Europe. Whose natural rhythm was it based on initially? Was it an authentic rhythm of a certain family or town? Does the rhythm even arise from a sense of biological rhythms, or could it possibly have been designed around an ideology?

Observing the productive results of the last two to three hundred years reveals that this rhythm does masterfully sustain certain outcomes: increased growth of revenue, GDP, and population, to name a few. It also promotes ideals ways (whether optimal or not) of moving the body, speaking, emoting, resting, eating, and even making love. These underlying statements, neither right nor wrong, seem to be woven into the practices of dominance culture: "Nature, if not tamed, will . . ."; "People, if left to their own devices, will . . ."; "If I follow my urges, I will . . ."; or "If I trust what feels natural, I will . . ." You could finish these sentences for yourself.

Breathing happens approximately sixteen times a minute, less frequently during meditative states, and at a higher frequency in children. A resting adult's heart rate can be anywhere from forty to eighty beats per minute. A hummingbird in flight has a heart rate of around three hundred beats per minute. When you watch an angiograph, you see blood vessels contract with pressure to move blood; hopefully, more pressure moves blood out of the heart compared to less pressure returning it to the heart. The body has other rhythms too. Craniosacral therapists are trained to feel deep fluctuations in the body, ranging from one to three to ten cycles per minute. With these fluctuations, your body encounters changes in shape and function as a result of returning into relationship with the greater world.

As mentioned in Chapter 1, the first rhythms, from conception through the first year of life, can shape your rhythm and nature for the rest of your life. Your rhythms will intelligently mimic and morph with your original conditions, be they life promoting or life threatening. The rate, frequency, and quality at which you are held, soothed, fed, and surrounded educate your cellular rhythms even when you're in the womb. If you remember the definition of recapitulation, once those baselines are established during your prebirth and birth periods, a dependency is created that you seek again later in life. Of course, as the fourth principle states, it is never too late to heal. Baselines can readjust to match your essential nature rather than your imprints. When you learn to recognize your rhythms, you lay the groundwork for your ability to comprehend the sentience of other living beings and give credence to the effects you have on them.

Remember, also, the third principle: Babies are the barometer. A baby's unrest might be a response to the unnatural rhythms of the adults around her. Adults must have a certain degree of authenticity in their rhythms if babies are to relax. Babies can't escape nature and react when and how they are asked to. They are barometers, signaling everything that belongs and anything that is missed from the support around them—or signaling objects in the field from previous generations. If a culture dominates its internal and external natural rhythms, its babies will cry out for them to be restored. The sensual world is their only language. Because they are born with well-articulated senses, culture may look to them as emissaries of nature and authentic rhythms.

Reclaiming the Body: The Path Home

If you can feel your body, you can learn to trust. Is this a bold comment? You may wonder how that works. Consider your body as a finely tuned barometer that can report back to you what you sense. Your body acts as a feedback mechanism, alerting you to how your world is affecting you and what it wants from you so you can make your next, most sustainable step.

But what if what you sense does not match what you are told you are sensing? Imagine you are blindfolded and asked to put your hand into a bag and identify what is in there. You reach in, and someone says to you, "These are grapes." Only your hand, once it touches the bag's contents, is sure these are not grapes but crushed bananas. What if you can actually smell the crushed bananas, even as you hear the word "grapes"?

Here is a more serious example: What if your father—or your mother, your child, pet, friend, or lover—has died? You're back at work because you've had three days off, and you're supposed to be done grieving, but all your body has to offer are tears. Do you decide that you're going to make it so three days *is* enough and you are "over it"? What if you're at work, at a restaurant, or supposed to be doing something, but you're crying helplessly? Or are you anxious? Or unable to speak? In this case, the choice to dominate the body's senses is understandable. But are you really "supposed to be" doing anything else besides crying and grieving in the company of others who are willing to grieve and cry with you? Imagine the degree of conflict you might be in.

What other ways could you deal with that conflict? Sedatives, analgesics, or other "soothers" can be helpful and delay the feelings from arising. Some humans can hold emotion back well enough and long enough that they become depressed. Imagine what happens when delaying grief has become a lifelong habit, learned from who-knows-how-many generations ago. What if what you sense (e.g., what your body's trying to deliver to you through physical sensations) and what is deemed "appropriate" are out of alignment? That conflict is going to show up in your body and in your behaviors. Your body will feel numbness, pain, agitation, hunching, clenching, stiffening, or collapsing. Behaviors might be violence or addictions.

Your body knows how to delay and will. It has the intelligence to get you somewhere safe before you discharge the stress, but if a "good time" for that discharge doesn't come soon enough (as it hasn't for much of the world living under real and perceived duress), it will show up instead in all sorts of unexpected places and manifestations—in the economy, world hunger, poverty, and cultural violence.

Besides the collective "build-up" of unprocessed grief in culture, and besides the changes in your body and in your behavior—as if those weren't enough—you will, most sadly, learn to distrust yourself and your body, your intimate link to joy.

Redefining Pain

Participants in a retreat I was leading were exploring alignment practices combined with yoga and meditation. The workshop included gentle awareness exercises that relaxed the feet, stabilized the core abdominal muscles, and created gentle supportive contact between participants. Many participants were experiencing pain. They were also feeling scared because they weren't sure where the pain was coming from and feared it would get worse.

Pain can be an unknown in that way. In this case, although each participant's pain had its own roots, all participants were united in one attribute: The pain was getting worse because they were afraid.

Once the retreat group realized that many were experiencing this phenomenon, they began a spontaneous dialogue about beliefs and pain. One participant was clear that, to her, pain meant "something is getting hurt." Another participant suggested, "There are different kinds of pain." She offered the example of childbirth, where "pain is a part of a natural process."

Pain is a message. Sometimes it is saying, "I'm getting hurt." And sometimes it's not. Today's culture is blessed to have sophisticated medical developments that assist in survival and pain relief. Pain suppressants are sometimes needed after surgery. Some women wish for the support that pain management offers during childbirth. In a chronic pain situation, like a disc protrusion, people ask for pain management, or they become depressed. Pain is exhausting.

My own grandmother, an active woman and one of the most loving human beings I have ever met, used to play tennis almost every day. Over the years, her hips became very sore. X-rays revealed degenerative joint disease in both her hips, and she was scheduled to have both hips replaced one year apart. The look of strain on her face every day during the months leading up to the surgery was memorable. The more pain she was in, the unhappier she became. After the surgery, the change was drastic. Looking in her eyes, I saw that the sparkle had returned.

"How are you?" I asked.

She exhaled. "It's so nice to not be in pain!"

There is a place for pain medication and pain management, but on many occasions an unopened gift awaits you inside pain. If you suppress pain long enough, your body loses vitality and clarity. The gift that's trying to reach you gets louder because your body, which loves you, makes the message louder. It may become so audible that it transforms into a diagnosable disease. Sometimes the messages must get that loud so they can be accurately detected.

When you dominate your senses, symptoms will show up all over your life, trying to point you back to living in a way that reflects your essential nature.

The next time you are stopped in your tracks because of pain, injury, or even a diagnosis, allow yourself to be struck with awe that your body considers you worth talking to. It's gotten your attention! Consider the compliment. You, the person in this perceived painful predicament, are wanted so badly by your being that it is trying to send you a message. Even though that message may be disturbing, it is the best way your being knows to reach you.

You may have habits other than being curious, like denying or becoming fearful or judgmental, that have been there for a long time. Don't become disheartened. Some people take their bodies to the gym, and before long their muscles relearn the habit of being strong. If you exercise open-mindedness, the muscle of your curiosity will strengthen too. The more you use it, the stronger it becomes.

The IRP described in the next chapter is a process that helps you sharpen your senses and your awareness of your body and all its messages. It opens up a whole new vocabulary to describe your observations as well as a more curious mind. Stepping into emergent language and sensing—and stepping away from dominance dichotomies of right/wrong, good/bad, and normal/abnormal—is the path to discovering your body's unopened gifts when there is pain.

Redefining Disease

Invite yourself to consider disease, like pain, to be a message. Enclosed in the message is an opportunity to follow a trail your essential nature has left for you. If you follow the trail, you will find your way back to your nature.

For example, do you know any women who have been diagnosed with breast cancer? Once they have felt shock, depression, and anger, a common epiphany women have is the realization: "I've been putting everyone else's needs ahead of mine. It's been as though what I need is not important. Now I'm going to think about my own desires." They have lived with the tension between the values of their conditioned upbringings to be "nice," "helpful," and "good"—which at the right place and time are natural—and their own desires and authentic responses to what they are sensing. The belief many women—and in fact, many people of both sexes—carry around goes something like, "I won't get love if I take care of myself," or "If I meet my needs, somebody else will get hurt." After enough years of resiliently sustaining double binds like these, something unsustainable finally arises.

With the diagnosis of a disease, the volume on your body's message has turned up loud enough to be heard. It is saying, "No." No to what? To the habits that previously were performed out of guilt, obligation, or dominance culture conditioning. With some deep sensing, or perhaps because they have nothing else to lose because the worst has already happened, people facing a serious diagnosis finally give their wishes permission to be granted. Disease can be a radical reformer that explodes into awareness when you are faced with extinction.

It seems that disease and hardship are handholds for exploring your essential nature. Could it in some ways be a gift to have your life run aground with symptoms that cannot be ignored? Could your body be an instrument of your essential nature saying, "Stop! I want to shine through, and there is no good reason it cannot be so"? Could those who give you news of your disease actually be loyal messengers of your essential nature rather than heartbreakers disproving your perceived immunity from tragedy?

Following the trail of your body's symptoms and diagnoses may not remove them entirely, but it will certainly give you a greater sense of intimacy with your essential nature and wholeness. Not only does feeling your body and interpreting its messages equip you with tools to approach your essential nature, but it also equips you to more accurately interpret signs and clues from nature, animals, and, yes, babies. And since all three are barometers of the whole, when you open your senses and your curiosity in the face of difficulty, you reunite with your ecosystem, making *yourself* sustainable. Curiosity in the face of *dis-ease* can make the journey tender and rich.

Reclaiming Grief

Emotions are the natural offshoot of sensing your body. They are some of the greatest gifts of sensual humanity. Depending on which arise, you may judge them as right/good/normal or wrong/bad/abnormal, but they are often practical signals from your body, alerting you to pleasure or danger. They are the vestiges of habits formed tens of millions of years ago, when sentient life forms learned to flee or fight in reaction to life-threatening circumstances. (Think back to the brain development described in Chapter 2.)

Dominance culture, in its most sincere attempt to survive, has habitually repressed emotion that might hint at an individual's vulnerability and as a consequence, has deregulated the healthy relationship between the reptilian and limbic reactions and the cerebrum. This is most obviously seen in oppressed and war-torn cultures, where inhabitants are in a state of survival and are engaged in profound violence. Take the following, for example:

- Since the British left Palestine and a Jewish state of Israel was created, Palestinians and Israelis have exchanged blows, vying for land and autonomy. Although groups have been successful at brokering communication and reconciliation at grassroots levels, authentic reconciliation has not reached government levels. Killing continues on both sides.

- Tribal tension between the Tutsi monarchy and Hutu majority erupted after the dissolution of the Tutsi monarchy and withdrawal of Belgian troops. The Hutu majority killed more than five hundred thousand Tutsis over one hundred days in Rwanda in 1994. Tribal intolerance continues today.
- Shortly after World War I, over one million Armenians were marched to their deaths in the desert at the hand of the Ottomans, a now defunct empire that was based in what is now Turkey. Since the fall of the Ottoman Empire in 1923, Turkey still cannot acknowledge the genocide of the Armenians.

There are many more examples. You could surely add your own on both global and local levels.

Many peoples and countries are not able to grieve, heal, or even feel because they are in persistent states of survival, famine, or war and must deny their suffering, which in turn perpetuates states of violence and conflict. The dominance culture approach to grief is that there's not time for it; grief slows its members down, makes them appear weak and a target for predation, much like its attitudes toward the needs of children. Children suffer in these griefless places as their subtle and gentle senses are met by hardened and resilient societies. The prevailing cortisol axes interrupt the nurturing tendencies that would be available to them if their mothers and fathers felt safe and were nurtured themselves.

The emergent culture, in contrast, invites countries and their peoples to be supported so they can encounter their authentic responses after the fight-or-flight impulse has been satisfied. Emergent culture encourages and enhances efforts to further incorporate the unintegrated grief persisting from these epic and ongoing exchanges. The expression of human emotion, especially grief, must be acknowledged and felt on individual, national, and world levels if healing and peace are to happen. The IRP, described in Chapter 5, is designed to gently and compassionately deconstruct the habit of dominating and repressing grief and other life-infusing emotions. The future vision is to accept both dominance and emergence intelligence as well as to integrate "compassion," "sentience," and "responsiveness and relationship to nature" as markers of a society's success alongside physical strength and success in enterprise. As vulnerability increases in value in homes, communities, and nations, greater emphasis will be placed on sentience, which must serve as fertile soil for coming generations. When their essential natures flourish, future children will have the fortitude to repair what has been broken in previous generations.

Relinquishing Dominance over Children

Looking back at child-rearing habits from the last few centuries, we see that some societies have a noticeable phobia of being "run" by their children. This is another inheritance of dominance culture's survival mode. Because we have repressed such practices as revering nature, sensing the body, and accessing vulnerable emotions, we are upset and afraid when we see them expressed by children. Perhaps we fear for the child and feel we must help him overcome these vulnerabilities. Perhaps we fear for ourselves, facing the temptation to let emotions and our essential nature flower again in ourselves. As a result, we fear what we see as the power of the child, who is closer to nature.

There is no need to reexplore why we fear and repress these emotions in ourselves. But logically, there is no possible way a child could ever dominate an adult. Think of it this way: If you have influence over what a child eats, whether the child sits in his or her own urine and excrement, or stays warm or cold, how could you find yourself in a "power struggle" with an infant or toddler? There is no such thing. It's obvious who has the power. Adults who think of a child as manipulative either are grossly underresourced themselves and lack adequate support to accomplish a task on behalf of that child or (and probably *and*) remember deeply inaccurate judgments placed on themselves as babies or children.

The Prototype

Babies are close to their essential nature. That's why they are one of the emissaries of emergence, barometers of sustainability. Their well-being or lack thereof reflects the conditions of their adults (with surprising specificity) and their society. If all people enter the world knowing and feeling they matter, then they have received the first necessary rite of passage to becoming human and, in turn, are likely to be rightful participants of Mother Earth as she receives them.

What is it that makes a person feel she matters? Is the onus solely on the parents to foster a climate of welcomeness and wantedness? Are families truly equipped to impart the welcoming message when they are largely underresourced by living alone yet appearing self-sufficient?

The Village

Think deeply about what your ideal welcoming might look like. How would you have liked to be welcomed? What is your song? Has anyone ever heard it?

These early rhythms, which resonate in the field, affected you as a developing zygote and set up expectations for how your life in the physical world was going to be. Maybe the messages you received from your parents match what you would have wished for. Maybe they are different.

Think of conception as a form of birth itself, of coming from one side to another, of changing from formlessness to form. Even before babies have words to communicate with or ears to hear with, the family field informs and sculpts their shape; molds their being, brain, and behavior; and determines how their essential nature will express itself through its form, the body.

Could society's method of bringing children into the world become one of the greatest contributors to ecological sustainability, albeit late in the game? From the very beginning of development, the field informs. Knowing that all informs one and that one informs back to all, generations of children consciously conceived, gestated, born, and raised in an emergent culture and an oxytocin axis would naturally care for their bodies, their peers, the planet they walk on, and, in time, the children they bear. As they grow, their social and business practices will also be emergent and, therefore, sustainable. Herein lies a culture shift.

What might it be like if all children entered the watery world of conception accompanied by the palpable certainty that they were wanted and had been prepared for? They matter to their parents, who have, through no small effort, done their best to repair their own imprinting and differentiated their identities from objects in their family field. They matter to their parents' surrounding community, a group of at least eight to twelve other adults who also wish for these children to come and who lovingly support the parents and each other. They also matter to the surrounding cultural systems.

In this ideal community, the economy thrives using practices that leave no trace of toxicity, poverty, or injury to its workers or to the planet. Education includes experiences with the natural world and the cultivation of the senses. Commercial practices show that each and every child, even if unknown personally to CEOs, managers, sales representatives, and other workers, is a ward to each and every member of that company. Governments are the same way. All adults act as stewards of every child, present and future. Babies in the womb and outside the womb, and children, are regarded as emissaries of an emergent world and integral interpreters of the needs of the planet and all inhabitants. Each member of the human race knows through his or her own corporeal experience what it is to matter and to be wanted.

It is through these felt senses that society ushers in another sustainable age. All members of society embrace their nascent ability to "birth" the next generation, who become discoverers and devotees of this emergent praxis and thus, by right, become participants of this wondrous planet again.

The *emerging family* is a network. It includes parents and children, but it also includes community members who, although not creating new families, have emerged from them and ensure that others are emerging. The emerging family, although inspired by arriving babies, also captures and fulfills what has lived on since conception in every sentient being: the sentience for the world around them, present and past, seen and unseen. There is the knowledge of being needed and of mattering. Like emergent culture, an emerging family is both a practice and an ideology that celebrates life living through the material and immaterial world. It is about you, taking your full place in society by expressing the gifts you're here to share. You may be close to a child, like a midwife, doula, or obstetrician, joining in the encounter of what a child brings to the room upon first entry. You may be a grandmother or grandfather, watching your lineage live on past you, a legacy that you fulfilled the dream of when you were born. You may be far away, unaware of this child yet somehow, by engaging fully in the gifts you are born with, are saying, "This is my piece that I add to caring for my world. This is how I express how I and everyone matters to the whole." And something about how you hold that awareness—because you sense that, in fact, not only are you *in* the network but you *are* the network—sustains you in the next step of your every moment.

The following section contains an inspiring example of a community that has readopted its old village ways despite the influence of dominance culture. It understands how each member creates the whole and is responsible for every other member.

Case Study: Lower Hutt, New Zealand

In the community of Lower Hutt, New Zealand, is an organization called the Family Centre. It services the Maori, Pacific Island, and Pakeha (European) peoples of the region.

As part of what the Family Centre calls "just therapy," it brings the entire community together around an issue any individual is experiencing. For example, if an adolescent boy has committed a crime, not only will he receive personal counseling, but he will also meet with the counselors and his family. Later, so he is not thrust back into a community that fails to understand his plight and has contributed to the reason the boy has committed the crime, the village is invited to gather in his name. Villagers sit together in a large house built for rituals, customs, and important tribal decisions. They believe that, somehow, the boy has separated from his roots and, essentially, himself. Thus the boy's behavior reflects an unspoken suffering befalling the entire village.

As the community filters into the hall, the conversation begins. First, the therapists speak about how they know this boy. They announce that he is beginning to uncover the personal and cultural roots of what has brought him to present-day, self-betraying behaviors.

The tribal chief spontaneously adds, "I remember the day you were born. It was at the time when the great storms were receding, bringing back the Kaimoana [seafood]."

A friend joins in the talk, saying, "We walked together when your father was sick. We would walk every night together; it must have been for two moons. You were only a boy, and I knew it would be hard for you later."

The grandmothers chime in, "You were a rascal when we chased you away from the kitchen when you would steal the cooling buns from the oven. You always pretended it was your sister." She continues, "The day I heard the owl outside our door, I knew death was coming. You being with me at that time, I sensed it might be you to carry much of the cost."

And then the boy's mother says, "When your Matua [father] first died, I was heavy with my own pain. I felt I had lost my identity, and I know I left you and your sister too much. When I saw you with the older boys, who too were alone in the world, I shamed myself for what I was letting happen. You are a brilliant and sensitive boy, and I am sorry my sadness took me away from the time when I could have been listening, there for you, for us."

On the community goes, remembering, storytelling, and talking of the boy as a member of the greater village, each owning their piece of his seeming crime. They speak the whole day together, reminding the boy of who he is beyond his present-day behaviors. It isn't until every person in the room feels they have said what they need to say that the meeting ends.

The wholeness exemplified by the Family Centre's repair has been forgotten in dominance culture and is being remembered in emergent culture. Dominance culture believes it's useful to sort out our problems, both physical and emotional, but to do so in private, with closed doors and confidentiality. Yes, privacy needs to be protected from judgment and stigma in culture. It also needs to be protected to build trust. But what if you were encouraged, after enough trust and experience had been established with your community, to face concerns and disappointments together, as the Maori, Samoans, and Pakeha work toward in Lower Hutt? What support and relief might there be if you embrace the degree of connectedness and inherent influence you have on who the others become?

This example from the Family Centre demonstrates the sophistication of ancient cultures and of emergent culture values. In particular, the community collectively takes responsibility for its members' criminal behaviors and so collectively participates in its members' rehabilitation. This type of ancient tribal wisdom hearkens to a time when humans did not consider themselves separate from the whole and from nature, a time when community understood itself as an ecosystem and the aberrant practices of one member were reflective of a systemic disharmony, calling on simultaneous individual and communal inquiries. Emergent culture's well-being, like that of indigenous cultures, is contingent on the well-being of all its members while in relationship with the natural world, seen and unseen. Emergent culture's cosmology remembers no separateness.

Summary

In a sense, dominance culture is disbanding naturally as emergent culture, which has been around in dissociated threads since before the Neolithic period, coalesces. Major differences between the two styles are that dominance culture tends to reject the cues spontaneously arising from nature and intuition and largely relies on the rational for its decision making. Emergent culture incorporates those cues in addition to the rational approach. By looking to nature, including the teachings from nonverbal living things like trees, animals, and babies—the emissaries of sustainable living—the world will adopt more strategic practices for longevity on this planet. By revering nature, sensing the body, redefining pain and disease, and accessing human emotion, society can then begin to relinquish its need to dominate all the living emissaries.

One map offered for your journey to fulfill the fourth principle is the healing perspective and practice of the Intuitive Recovery Project. *Intuitive* because it is through relinquishing dominance, opening the senses, and accepting what is sensed that babies and all nonverbal beings will have their intelligence received.

PART THREE

The Marriage

CHAPTER 5

The Intuitive Recovery Project

And the day came when the risk it took to remain tight in a
bud was more painful than the risk it took to blossom.

—Anaïs Nin

*You may want to have a writing utensil and a piece of paper nearby as you
read this chapter.*

The Intuitive Recovery Project (IRP) can be used to facilitate any
transformation. It can be used in decision making and in healing diseases,
pain, or emotional heartbreak. It can also be used to decode the secrets in
your early experiences. This chapter gives you a version of the IRP you can
use on your own at home. You can use it for yourself but also as a tool for
decoding the secrets in the lives of babies. Decoding your secrets is one
of the best steps you can take to successfully understand any other being.

The Anatomy of the Intuitive Recovery Project

You may find this chapter reads like a protocol. It is intended that way, and
simultaneously, it is not. If you have ever attended an educational insti-
tution that teaches skills or vocations, you'll have been walked through
protocols to ensure you properly execute your designated task. For example, medical programs do an excellent job of standardizing protocols for
patient treatments because professional integrity and, to a large degree,

treatment success ride on previously agreed-on methods. Even though mastery of any healing art involves the use of intuition, teaching the student begins with protocols. *Protocols* can be thought of as trail markings that lead the student along the route to the river that is the medicine. Protocols are compasses that, with luck, place the student—and later the practitioner—near where he or she is most likely to enter the wisdom of the body's healing capacities. Protocols likely arose from other people's intuitive successes and accidental discoveries.

The IRP, although a protocol of six steps, is designed to be dropped once you have learned it and are comfortable with it. It is a trail, but you will eventually find your openings in the forest that take you to the most powerful places in the river. Once you know where you are, and you're not afraid to get lost because you've been walking beside the river for some time and have relearned how to trust your intuition, you can enter the river—the medicine—through your own means. The protocol is not to be mistaken for the medicine itself.

Challenges arise for many who are highly trained in their respective trades: business, health care, education, and others. Although practitioners never forget the core studies and techniques they are taught, once school finishes and several years of practice go by, innovation naturally starts to happen. Some practitioners feel more related to traditional teaching; others can't help but deviate as a new branch of wisdom begins growing out through them. This is all to say that you can be trusted to know what is right for you. The IRP is here to return your trust in yourself.

The IRP is not a replacement for medical, scientific, or professional training in the healing arts. It is, however, your birthright, one that may have been "taught" out of you by living in the dominance culture—hence the word *recovery.* I found that, once I started using the IRP, patients in my practice were better able to show me what was at the root of their *dis-eases.*

The Marriage of Science and Experience Revisited

Go back to the myth of Science and Experience. Recall how neither Science nor Experience felt complete without the other. Each on their own shore, they longed for something more, not even knowing they were longing for the other. Both did their best to feel complete despite the longing, and despite the separation, they were both successful at contributing to those around them.

Much like these mythic characters, you live in a world that is divided. Science has taught what society needs to know about the structure of the human body (anatomy), how its mechanisms work (physiology), and how things can go wrong (pathology). Experience passed down to us from ancient cultures has taught us how to anchor medicinal practices in nature, the animal world, and the unseen world of intuition. Complete knowledge comes from the Great Marriage between their two worlds: Science and Experience. *This Great Marriage starts inside you.* The marriage begins back at the place when your wholeness was first divided. So since division has been going on for a long time, you can assume there is work to do. Society is in *recovery.*

Think of the information in this book as a marriage between scientific data and intuitive experience, between the wisdom that has arisen from discoveries during world history and the knowledge gained as a result of its mistakes. Think of this book as an invitation to blend the benefits of dominance culture with intuition and a relationship with the natural world in order to create an emergent culture. The reunion out of separateness happens with the implementation of intuition. Science places you, your family, and your community somewhere near where you are likely to find your medicine. You are on the path. Intuition, or Experience, is the direct route to the river, to the medicine. Together, Science and Experience rekindle the wholeness, and that is where the medicine reenters your body, your heart, and your relationship with all sentient and nonsentient beings. There you find your essential nature, where unity is your only experience.

Remember the moment when Science lets the water carry him out to the middle of the sea? He has no proof that it's the right thing to do. Logically, he has neither data to stay on the shore and continue searching for "more" nor data to follow the unreasonable call out into the waves. What breaks the "tie" is that he can't help himself. Although he doesn't recognize it, his intuition has pulled him into a decision. He makes it from an entirely different state of mind than he's used to. It is the sound of his lover's voice that reunites him with his *knowing*. His illogical yet long-standing sense that "there is something more" only makes sense to him once he recognizes the sound of his long-lost lover's voice. Science's pursuit of data to confirm his logic is abandoned and no longer needed once his intuition takes over.

Experience, on the other hand, is wholly in her feelings. Her senses are alive in the work she does, and she has no need to think, rationalize, or even communicate what she knows. She stumbles in her work, though, because she is challenged to communicate what she knows to others, giving them the skills to heal themselves. She longs for help to impart her message and doesn't remember that she once had her other half who could do that on behalf of her senses. She barely knows what is missing but senses there is "more." Once she sees the face of her long-lost lover reflected in the waves, a thought forms, an unfamiliar event, but because it compels her forward and she is practiced in the art of trust, she pursues the thought.

The Irony of Intuition

The continual irony of intuition is that it rarely makes logical sense to follow it. But contained within it is a surprising amount of intelligence, a combination of thinking, logic (or not), sensing, and feeling. When you look back later, you feel surprisingly confirmed that it did provide the best outcomes, perhaps even surpassing your expectations.

Because intuition also holds the keys to fulfillment, following it reunites you with your essential nature, joy. The IRP is one way to retrieve essential wholeness and joy.

Here are some examples of life with and without intuition. If you have worked without intuition, then you have experienced the following:

- frustration when you were in pain
- unwillingness to rest when you were tired
- repression of or overindulgence in your hunger
- lack of trust that others can or want to care for you

When you embraced your intuition, you experienced the following:

- curiosity when you were in pain
- creativity when things did not look like they were going your way
- responsiveness to your body's requests for self-care
- willingness to be vulnerable, fallible, and humble
- other experiences (you may have a list that comes to mind)

I hope that once you have gone through the IRP, you will also experience the following:

- renewed compassion in the face of your or another's suffering
- renewed capacity to access feelings and restoration of equanimity in the face of challenging situations
- enhanced ability to let messages from your external and internal environments (including from your body sensations and emotions, and from babies, animals, and nature) conavigate your decision making

One thing to remember is this: Your body never lies. It doesn't need to. Your body has one agenda: life. The life it wishes for you is one of wholeness. Consider your body a barometer, just like a baby, from which you will receive feedback in the form of sensations and circumstances that reflect various degrees of balance and imbalance. Trust your body, and as you explore the IRP, you will find balance.

The Protocol

The IRP is the result of nature. It belongs to no one. It arises out of the river where the medicine is. It is born into the world and into human beings and is taught by the body and all living things. It has a name only to transmit its wisdom into words.

Also for the sake of transmission, it is introduced here as a protocol that, if followed, will deliver an outcome for you—but it is also a practice.

For the sake of organization, the IRP is offered in six distinct stages, a series of steps that describes a specific pathway during a healing event:

1. Connection
2. Detection
3. Intentions
4. Resources
5. Protectors
6. Access

You may find that, once you read about them and try these steps, you prefer to place them in a different order or even use different words. The healing and maturing process in life does not always move in a specific order. Use *your* river's language.

The IRP is short. At most it may span two hours, but it can also happen in seconds, once you are adept at it. There is no end and no beginning.

The exercises suggested in this book are by no means exhaustive; they are merely an introduction to what is a more extensive training that runs over several years. Because you, like all life, are dynamic, you cannot go through life without being subjected to the forces of change. Moving with them and allowing your being to reconcile with the forces creates and maintains vitality and health. Resistance, although it may be an innocent attempt to maintain love and health, leads to discomfort and even disease. You're not meant to get life "right" or to "keep things together"; you are only encouraged, here in the IRP, to be responsive to your senses while staying as connected as possible to your essential nature.

Dominance culture has not passed this skill on to succeeding generations, so it makes sense that we must recover our ability to connect to the wholeness of life. In the wholeness, intuition is present, and it is through the connection with all life that intuition can be trusted, because information about the present moment and what is being asked for next arises from the totality. Sensing, feeling, and responding to information arising from your senses make you dynamic. Blocking any sensing, feeling, and responding brings on discontent and dis-ease from being unresponsive. Think of the IRP as relearning how both the water and the riverbed are changed by meeting. It happens on the micro level of your cells and on the macro level in the universe, with personal and societal relationships. It is amid one thing and many things.

Pulling the Thread

The IRP can be used to heal your greatest hurts or to enhance an already healthy life. You may also find that some of the steps are helpful when you encounter an impasse with your partner, children, friends, or work colleagues.

Although it's often easier to notice other people's patterns, you might already be aware that you have behavioral habits or patterns, physical or emotional, that you or others don't especially like. You may even feel your habits or patterns are not in your control, or they may have you feeling repeatedly a victim of circumstances caused by others.

The four principles described in preceding chapters might have alerted you to the possibility that some of your patterns have very old origins. Because patterns or sequences are known to repeat over generations and across cultures, you may be initiating a recovery process that is a complex of hundreds, if not thousands, of years. The IRP is going to have you grasp those patterns as the present-day end of a thread reaching back to the earlier challenge that created the symptom. When you start pulling the thread, you may be surprised at how long it is. It may stretch back into your very early life, where your brain, behaviors, and body were first shaped. By slowly and lovingly pulling the thread and using the IRP, you can transform the degree of power the unwanted pattern has over your life. Decoding and unraveling your patterns gives you more choice about how much your history affects you in the present.

Exploring the center of the spool, the earliest lessons you received, is a tricky task. It's an emergent practice. This means that slowing down and opening your senses will help. Your learned habit likely developed when you were moving much slower than you do today, so it makes sense that, in order to access it and recover your essential nature from underneath it, you must slow down so you can meet up with your earlier self. After the IRP, you may decide you like a slower pace and can enjoy your life more at that speed.

Based on what you read in earlier chapters, it may have occurred to you that your present-day unwanted symptoms arise from experiences you had as a baby, even if you don't "remember" them. Although the prebirth and birth periods are not always the first time you learned your habits, those time periods may arise during the IRP. It is one of the most intriguing times in life because that's when the most rapid learning happens. Humans are born "half-baked" and completely reliant on relationships with their environment to guide the stages of development that come next, and this reliance lasts for up to eighteen to twenty years. Because babies, unlike most other mammals, do not walk at birth, every moment of learning gives directions for how limbs, organs, facial expressions, hormonal secretions, bowel habits, sleep cycles, and more can best perform for optimum survival in the presenting environment.

This slow world of your early experiences is rich and young, full of sensations and feelings. Can you guess why there are few words? The experiences that first shaped you happened before you coordinated the language centers of your brain. This is why, if you feel rushed or urgent, or even if you try to use your thoughts to get from the outside of your thread to the center of your spool, you might miss the magic.

Inquiry as a Spiritual Practice

Remember back to the discussion of imprinting in Chapter 1. Every person has been imprinted by challenging events and circumstances, both wanted and unwanted. Although it is uncomfortable, being imprinted by unwanted experiences is a divine process of unfolding in your lifetime, a divine right. You may feel like you are alone as you begin your IRP process. This is a common response that comes from the reality that you are alone, and you're making a big change. But even though you are alone, you can recruit the natural world, the animal world, and other human allies while you deepen your path.

People you once thought to be your closest allies may not like the changes you are making. They may want you to stay as you are. Although their concern appears to be about you, their wishes actually have nothing to do with you at all. They may not want you to change because they are unable to acknowledge that they, too, are alone on their path. It's a tough pill to swallow. You are putting your pursuit of intimacy with yourself over the expectations others might have of you. As you uncover layers of dominance culture–taught ways of being, notice how you free yourself to be more of who you are.

My patients have reported that, until going through IRP, "I didn't know I wasn't living my full life." It's OK to want more intimacy and love in your life. You might be happier giving yourself permission to ask for it.

Close your eyes and breathe in deeply. Notice the stillness there. Exhale. You've read a lot of information up to now. You've explored one side of the marriage. Now a different side will take over. Stand as close as you can to the river. It's time for your story. Your body knows exactly what to do. It has always known.

The Project

Step One: Connection

Connecting is a decision. There are many stimuli in your world worthy of your attention. So what are you making a connection with? Does connection mean you should find something to touch? To stare at? You touch, stare at, and think about many things every day. You're already connecting, right?

The answer is yes, you are already connecting with the everyday aspects of your life, the joys and struggles, and its physical objects and people. The kind of connection you're making in this step, however, is to the subtle, underlying presence woven through and between all your body's tissues. Even though all religious, spiritual, and scientific traditions have a name for this underlying presence—God, nature, the universe, creation, the soul, and so on—you don't have to name it unless you want to.

Why would you want to connect with the underlying presence in your body? Connection is a mental and physiological state of being. It can provoke a sense of well-being and contentment; on the other hand, if sensations arise that are uncomfortable, connection can be aggravating or even scary. Regardless of the quality of sensation, it is a state of "intimacy." You can feel it while you are at rest, at work, or even during a stressful circumstance. Eventually, with enough practice, you can stay connected during challenging circumstances, so that even when a storm is all around you, you are standing in the spacious and centered eye of it. Connection has the following effects on you:

- Your nervous system feels like you are in a zone of flexibility and ease, which you notice in your relaxed mood and body.
- Your body temperature is at a comfortable level.
- Your breathing is relaxed and your ribs and back are moving.
- Your mood is patient and attentive to what is afoot.

As a result, your awareness feels clear and sharp. You are sensing smell, sound, taste, body, and heart. What enters your awareness may be challenging, but it is nonetheless welcome. Your ability to communicate is heightened, and your ability to connect authentically to yourself or those around you is enhanced.

Feeling connected to yourself signals to the living world around you that you are available, that you have reconnected to the world. Plants, animals, and babies will notice your connectedness. You will practice sensing plants, animals, and babies. You will practice sensing your essential nature, that which you hold in common with all living things.

The Practice

Sit quietly.

Although there are many things on your mind, and you have responsibilities, for the next several minutes, stop the clock.

There may be sounds and thoughts all around you. Hear the empty space between them. Find the edge of your riverbed. Even the emptiness has a sound.

Place your attention between the sounds, between the sensations in your body, and between what you see in front of you or in your mind's eye.

Find the emptiness. It's a place too.

Your body and being know how to do this. And your only decision is whether you want to notice what arises.

This might be all you want to do. Sit for a few minutes. Listen to your sensations. Notice how rich a world of feedback is right there at your first glance. If you want to go further,

Thank yourself for having the courage you have in this moment. You could be in many other moments, but you've chosen this one. Look around you. Notice the structures that make the place you're in a place. Are there floors or walls? Grass, sand, or trees? Acknowledge the structures that support your body from the inside and from the outside right here in this moment. Acknowledge their participation and involvement.

Connection is a meditative process. If you would like to learn more, consider exploring the meditative techniques in your particular religious, spiritual, or healing tradition. Connection can happen at all times. You can enter, move through, and exit your day sensing and noticing, alone and in all your relationships with the living world.

You can repeat connection anytime, anywhere. You may even want to record your voice reading the italicized words from this section and play the recording back as you meditate and connect. Or you might create your own words to lead you into connection.

Connection is the first step of the IRP. Unlike the situation when you go to a therapist's office or a workshop, you are invited to be both the facilitator and the patient. You are invited to be both the child and the parent. It is from a place of relative connection that you are best equipped to be the facilitator/"good" parent.

Step Two: Detection

In this step, you will detect and articulate a challenge you experience in your present day and follow it with techniques to better understand where it comes from and how to lovingly integrate it back into wholeness.

Why focus on what's challenging? Contained in your challenges are kernels of wholeness. There is no difficult moment, feeling, or circumstance that is devoid of wholeness. So take this opportunity to consider the habit or pattern in your present that has truly been challenging you. It may be a recent development, or it could be something you've known about for some time.

One way to detect your present-day challenge is to recall a response you have that seems irrational given the circumstances it arises in. It could be fear, a physical sensation, a desire to run, or a belief about yourself or another—there are many possibilities. Next, notice that you likely don't tell anyone about your habit when it's happening; you may even go to great lengths to conceal it. You may now sense an inkling of the feeling that you are thinking about it. You may have words, or possibly a shape, for it. You may only have a feeling, with no words and no shape. Let your knowledge of your present-day challenge arise enough that you are reminded of it now.

The Practice

Take the words, shape, or feelings that accompany your challenge and put them on a page.

Take a couple of minutes until you can feel spaces in between your thoughts and sensations. Connect.

How do you describe the reaction you have that seems irrational or out of control when it's happening—so much so that even when you look around and can see that it is not happening, you nonetheless expect it to happen? Write it down.

When you're ready, ask and do your best to answer the question: Where in my body do I feel my pattern?

Take your time and wait until it becomes a sensation. Even if you've never had experience with this, do your best to have faith that your body is wise and stores information.

This step may last several minutes. When you have the answer, write it down or draw it next to your detection. Then ask yourself: What general age does my body feel like it was when I first learned this habit?

You may see your size and relate that to a stage of life. You may get a number. Write down what arises.

Notice what first flashes to your awareness. You may find multiple answers arise. Usually the first one is the closest.

If you can't trust what's arising, that's OK. Maybe you don't need to know. You can always return to this practice later and try again. You may want to break each step down and do them only one at a time.

Whatever does come to awareness, write it down in a form as close as possible to what arose in your mind. Even if you think it's "nothing." Write it down.

Put aside your paper with your detected pattern, where you feel it in your body, and your general age the first time you learned it. You'll return to this page soon.

Step Three: Intentions

Once you have connected and detected, it's a good time to identify your intention. Intention is a focusing rod for your IRP. Your intention is related to what you'd like to get out of this experience.

Your intention might be as general as "I welcome the best outcome possible" or maybe something more specific. Examples could include the following:

- I want to improve on . . .
- I would like to become more aware of or get in touch with . . .
- I would like to get to the root of this pattern . . .

Humans are good at explaining what isn't working and what they don't like about how they are feeling. "I don't like that my leg hurts; I want it to stop." Identifying negatives is easy: "I don't want my leg to hurt." Stating your wishes positively takes more thought and requires that you explore how things could be: "I would like to feel comfort and ease in my leg."

Intentions are states of being or experiences you would like to have that support your optimal state of being. Sometimes it helps to first know what you don't want, because from there you can articulate what you do want. So start wherever it's easiest, but make sure you end up stating what you want more of. Make sure that, if you achieved your intention, you would feel nothing short of joy. Shoot high.

The "something not working" may be an emotional symptom, such as anxiety, depression, or inertia; it may be a physical symptom, such as pain, imbalance, or a disease diagnosis; or it may be a situational symptom, such as a recurring pattern at work, in relationships, or in things that happen to you. Any and all these can be considered for exploration.

These may be some of your symptoms:

- consistent pain or disappointment in a place in your body
- repetitive destructive or disappointing patterns in your relationships

- prevailing emotional feelings, beliefs, or fears

You may have doubts about the possibility of being at your best, and you will have quick access to material that can prove your doubts are real. That has nothing to do with your best. Yes, moments in your past have formed your doubts, but are they happening now?

Your intention, in contrast, is the dream of who you are underneath all that happened. There is a place—your wholeness, your essential nature— that was never touched by past events and has always been intact. You know it's there. You may only know it by knowing the idea, but it is there.

The Practice

Sit and welcome connection back into your attention.

Take a couple of minutes until you sense spaces of nothingness, where you have relinquished the habit of working hard at anything.

Remember your detection. Think about where you have been and where you are going in regard to your detected habit or pattern. Imagine yourself at your best in regard to it.

Now ask your wholeness or your essential nature how you want to feel once you have used the IRP to transform your detection.

Expand your imagination. Reach the edges of your thoughts out farther than they have ever been allowed to go before. Imagine yourself fully inhabiting the space of that expansion.

Notice the interruptions that come to distract you while you are expanding. Take them as they are and lovingly fold them into your expansion, like a good parent, taking them with you. Interruptions are not who you are.

Reach to the edge of your imagination, bringing all of yourself with you. This is where your intention for how you'd like to feel regarding your present habit/pattern lives.

Set your intention clearly into a feeling, an image, or a phrase. Put it down on paper.

"I'd like to feel/be/have ..."

If you like words, name the outcome that improving a quality, becoming more aware of your habit, or getting to the root of your pattern will lead to. If you prefer images, draw a picture that shows you embodying your intention. If it's more of a feeling, conjure up the sensation that resembles how you feel when your intention is realized.

Be confident that focusing your attention on your intention will cultivate an outcome. Thoughts are powerful organizers of actions. This is why having a clear intention is vital to your IRP.

Don't be concerned if no one else would understand the meaning of your intention's words, images, or feelings. You understand it. Often your deepest intention is the very first thought, image, or feeling that flashes through your mind when you are asked, "What would you like?"

Take in these words of reassurance: Once you have found words, images, or feelings for your intention, know that your intention is already coming to fruition. You would not have been able to dream the dream of your intention unless, in some way, it was already in motion. Now that you have heard, seen, or felt your intention, experience the IRP begin to move you toward it.

Step Four: Resources

Your resources are inborn, intact, already-healed, and never-been-hurt places in your being. They are felt senses and ways of being that most closely resemble you when you come into contact with your essential nature. They are what you want to feel like more often. They are glimmers of what life has been like from time to time when your life flowed, when you felt connected, or when you were "on your game."

You may remember the day you last felt your resources. It may have been right before a large disappointment, a surgery, or an injury. It may have been just before something happened to someone you love. Deep down, underneath any unwanted circumstance or shock you've been through, you still have your resources. In this step, you relocate them and get back in touch with them so they are available to you as you move forward.

Why do you need resources? What do they have to do with intuition? Resources are your anchor. They remind you that your essential nature is intact and whole under any hurts or imprints you've collected in your life.

If you establish a connection to your resources before going further into the IRP, you will find it easier to link to them when you encounter more challenging circumstances. There are moments during the IRP process when you will have intense emotional or physical sensations. At those times you may feel fear or pain. This is when you need your resources. You'll want to use them when you find yourself coping by going numb, feeling overwhelmed, or feeling physical pain, anxiety, fear, or sadness. (Depending on the early events that shaped your coping strategies, you will be more prone to one or another style of coping.)

Even with all your preparation, however, there may be times when the sensations you have during the process are so strong that you need other resources and supports. Some people breathe; others think about pressing their feet into the ground; others remind themselves that they are not alone and that other people are working on similar problems in the world. This might be a good time to book an appointment with a trusted practitioner or to turn to a trusted friend or to your partner. Maybe it's just time to take a break or make tea. A resource is whatever settles you into a perspective that has you feeling like you are "OK," "able to do it," "not alone," or in neurological terms, in "a regulated state."

The Practice

Sit and think about your resources.

Ask yourself, What is it like when I deeply trust myself?

There will be layers. Start with the layer that first comes to your attention. Note it. Acknowledge the sensation, image, or thought.

Ask again, What is it like when I deeply trust myself? *Notice the layer that arises in your attention.*

Sit with the layers.

You may wonder if you can trust the layers. See about resting in the most stable, comprehensive, and calming layer.

Notice the layers that have been shaped and the ones that are unable to be shaped. All the layers have played different roles.

Now recall your intention. Look at the piece of paper where you wrote it down, conjure up the felt sense of what it will be like when it is realized in your life.

The role of your intention is to retrain you so you can spend more time in the felt senses that most serve you and make you feel whole. Your resources know how to bring you to your intention.

You're now going to bring your intention and your resources together. Here's how:

Let's pretend your intention is to live your life with the same kind of pleasure you get from "xyz." If you can't think of an ideal state, then try to imagine one of the best times of your life:

- *Conjure up the memory of what it was like the last time you tasted that ideal state. Imagine the way your body felt, the look on your face, and how you treated others.*
- *Now remember the sensation you felt. Where do you feel it in your body when you remember it? Your mouth? Your stomach? Do you feel the presence of the sensation anywhere else? Take note of the sensation. Notice how it makes your body feel. How do you feel about yourself?*
- *Now just focus on the sensation. What do you discover? If you are able to maintain the sensation, then you are tapping into the sensation of your endorphins mixed with some oxytocin. (Remember, that's the love hormone you learned about earlier.)*
- *What you're doing is positively imprinting yourself with resources while reminding yourself that the sensation is yours to access whenever you wish. If you've ever waited for a resourcing circumstance to come your way so you could feel well, you can now see that you are able to create a resourced state and bring it to any circumstance you want.*

What if you believe you have never experienced a resourced state? How, then, would you conjure up a resource sensation? How do you conjure up a sensation you've never had?

Resource sensations can also come from how you believe it feels to have pleasure (or for that matter, how it feels to have ease, equanimity, joy, and peace). The sensation is within you; the conjuring of the sensation awakens the memory of it. You can invoke it. Conjuring up and sensing your resources is a leap of faith.

Try this practice for finding resources even if you have no remembered sensation for them. You can invite your body to share a resourced sensation with you anyway. If it works for you, keep using it. You can also make up your own practice that reminds you of your resources.

Stand. Using your mind's eye, trace the boundaries around your body.

Feel the gravity of your body where you stand. Notice the surfaces that support your weight. Feel where they and your body meet. Notice the pressure.

Wait. Get heavier. Ask your tailbone to become heavy, as though a weight is hanging from it, down between the inside of your heels.

Seek to extend the gravity of your lower body so that it sinks at least a meter into the earth beneath the ground. Find your natural anchor there.

Be patient. There is an anchor, a place where your energy runs continuous with Earth.

Take your attention away from your gravity.

Breathe. Notice a few breaths.

Take your attention away from your breath and feel around. What's there? What's within you? Around you? How big are you, really?

In this place, notice your predominant feeling. Is it quietness? Stillness? Love? Something else, maybe unsettling? Boredom?

You are connected to the Great Mother, Mother Earth. The Mother's body is calm, warm, and welcoming.

Scan between the right and left sides of your body, between the front and back, from the top to the bottom.

Feel the inside of your body. Move your attention to the outside of your body, and then from the outside back to the inside.

Rest now.

What feels whole? Right? Expansive?

Linger there.

These sensations are resources. Invite them to form a gentle container around every sensation, every emotion, and the space around your body, your home, your community, and the planet.

You might need practice to feel centered and resourced. Trust that you know how, even if it's been a long time since you last felt this way. If you don't think you've ever felt your resources, you can set your intention to be something like, "I want to feel what it feels like to have resources."

I recommend getting a clear sense of your resources before embarking on the next series of healing steps. Take as long as you need.

Naming an intention and finding ways to resource yourself align you with your oxytocin axis. Your intention and resources act as navigators to guide you along the often winding, and at times disorienting, healing process. No matter where you are within your IRP, you can use your intention to remember why you are doing this process. If the process becomes challenging or uncomfortable, use your resources. There is no rush and no right way to do the IRP. The most important factor to keep in mind is to go at your own pace and to do it with patience, compassion, but most of all, integrity, which is another way of saying, "Do it *your way.*"

Step Five: Protectors

Protectors of childhood wounds stand like sentinels at the gate of your most defenseless treasures. They sprang up a long time ago, when an event crossed your path that you perceived to be life threatening. Clearly, you did not die, although it may have felt like you came close. And maybe you nearly did die. At the time, this feeling was larger than your ability to reason with it. Perhaps no one noticed you were going through this event and experiencing this feeling, and as a result, you were not comforted. Despite that, you decided you would survive. Human beings have an incredible will to live. It was at that moment that your body performed a great act on your behalf: It took the feeling of being about to die and, just before you felt the full brunt of it, quickly stored it away in a safe place somewhere in your body.

It's a strange phenomenon that feelings of rejection, abandonment, and isolation are coupled with, or rather precipitate, anticipation of death. Depending on how young you were when you encountered any of those three feelings, they would have been synonymous with death because your survival completely relied on being secure with the adults taking care of you.

Because your body is a great protector of your life, in its compassionate wisdom it protects you from frightening sensations like fear of imminent death. Rather than allowing you to encounter the fear, your body's wisdom quickly shuttles it into the most suitable place in your body and begins to build a wall around that place until you feel adequate safety through sustained comfort. This wall building is your body's way of helping you survive. It is an act of love.

As the wall is built, one by one your systems join in to guard the wall. Your nervous system is asked to raise its watch, and it goes from a well-regulated code blue of an integrated cortex, limbic system, and reptilian brain to the code yellow or red, in which the reptilian brain and limbic system go into survival mode and the cortex strategizes best survival tactics. Your muscles respond and prepare themselves for striking or running, or in the absence of those options, for freezing. The nerves hold the muscles like puppet strings, feeding them repeated messages: "Stay alert; you need to watch what's happening around you in case this happens again."

After years of this alert, your brain, body, and behaviors have all come to expect these messages, and your posture begins to organize around the messages, as if they were a stone in the river. Your shoulders may hunch, your lower back may sway, your hips may turn, or your jaw may set forward, backward, or sideways.

Then there are your organs. They might respond by acting like the nerves that supply them, tensing and contracting. They may experience futility and become underactive. Your organs are the deep holding tanks of your emotions and your power. Think of them as caverns that inform the shape of your body, sheltered within the walls (bones) of the castle. The caverns are the toughest places for invaders to get to, so they are often the place where the overwhelming feelings you felt a long time ago have been tucked away. Sometimes even the fluids of the body, such as the cerebrospinal fluid, carry the imprints of your early challenging experiences. In this case, your spine and its muscles are called in to wall the sensations off from your awareness, to dutifully protect you from their effects.

Cultural and spiritual traditions have designed sacred architecture around the body metaphor. Most traditions around the world and throughout history have a version of the protected treasure:

- The ancient Jews have the story of their Holy of Holies, the innermost room of the temple said to contain the essence of the Creator.[1]
- Hindus have the Garbha, which in Sanskrit means the "womb chamber" or "innermost sanctum," where the primary deity of the temple resides.[2]
- Medieval castles were built with a tower in which survival essentials such as food and water were kept.[3] The tower was used as a safe house for nobility, who at the time were considered to be nearest to God.
- Ancient metallurgists built caves in the shape of a vulva in which they heated and smelted metals. They knew metals came from Mother Earth, and that she too must guide how they are used in society. They never entered while she worked, only checking her progress from outside the cave.[4]

Your essential nature has been referred to as being the equivalent of the Holy of Holies. What exactly is this *essential nature?* It's not your personality, the "you" that knows what kind of clothes you like to wear and what your favorite food is. It's not your emotions, the feelings you have, such as happiness, sadness, and frustration. It is not your body, your build, the color of your eyes, or your height. Your essence connected to your body a long time ago, probably around the time you were conceived. (The conversation about how that happens is worthwhile but won't be explored here.) You know you are feeling your essential nature when you feel whole.

Your body, with its protectors, will stop at nothing to defend your essence, your inner sanctum, your Holy of Holies. Your protectors shielded the intersection where life breathes your essence into your body and keeps it safe where it is now housed.

The IRP is a purification process. Instead of using sacred oils and years of devotional prayer—or maybe in addition to those practices—you enter into your sacred spaces by opening your senses. What vehicles will take you there? First, you will have to negotiate with your protectors. Your tools are compassion, courage, and your human senses.

How to Recognize Protectors

Some of your present-day behaviors are relics from when you were first hurt. They come out when you think you will be injured in a similar way. Many people don't make the connection. There are good reasons for this. The original experience, the imprint, is out of view. You don't know it's there. That's how skilled your body's wisdom was way back then. It knew how to get it away from your awareness fast enough so you wouldn't have to feel it. All living beings have this skill. It is life preserving and intelligent.

Unfortunately, society doesn't teach you that your present-day challenges have ancient roots. So when your protectors are triggered because an event in the present reminds them of the past, you are largely unaware of this memory. Your entire being, from your brain and your behaviors to how you bond, is being recruited to protect you from death or something close. You may be aware that you are having an irrational response to the present situation, but for some reason, you cannot stop it. It may even intrigue you. How is it you can be compelled to react even when you don't really want to or need to? Amazing.

Steps two and three of the IRP align your intention for how you'd like to feel instead of how your conditioned responses (your protectors) make you feel and act. And when you've located your resources, you can slowly begin to retrain your protectors to stand down and let you be more connected to your resources and your essential nature.

Generally, when people become aware of how they are protecting themselves in a situation, their first sensation after the awareness is shame. *I feel horrible to think that I am . . .*

- not in control
- possibly hurting someone
- embarrassed or alarmed that I didn't see this before

Notice what sensations come up when you become aware of your style of protection. It may be that your protectors will want to turn on even more strongly. They may want to bury your awareness in an avoidance habit, such as food, work, social media, or television. You may find it funny or unimportant. You may even feel like you have no answer for the question about protection style. If this is the case, consider reading "Step Five: Protectors" again later.

The Practice

Think about the body parts that seem to bother you often.

Think about the words you say to yourself when you are faced with a challenge.

Think about what your posture does when you are confronted by certain life circumstances. These are your protectors.

How do your protectors act?

Write down your protective behaviors beneath where you've written your intention.

Your first protectors were created when you were a child, even a baby in the womb, maybe even at conception. In this case, when you enter into the IRP, your compassion is offered to the child you once were. Although parents were most likely doing the best job they could, what often happens at the beginning of the IRP process is that you discover either that no one knew you were hurting or that you were insufficiently comforted when you were hurting. You felt disconnected from love. This does not mean that there were no doting adults around or that your parents were not doing their job. It may simply mean that the language you were using was not understood. As a result, your protectors did the job that your caregivers, often for innocent reasons, were unable to do. Your protectors cared for you by buffering the overwhelming sensations into walled-off areas of your body.

To be clear, this process of compassion is not about blaming others for your pain. It is true that some parents and caregivers have caused their children harm, as in an abuse situation or when they have neglected to comfort and care for their children.

Your protectors would not have had to develop unless there was reason for them to do so. Imagine a child or baby who is hurting, feeling disconnected from love, or alone. What would you do for that child? Most people are challenged to be compassionate to themselves at the beginning of the IRP. You might want to begin practicing compassion to the child you once were by first extending your compassion to an imaginary child or baby or maybe to one you already know and love.

See a room; notice the walls, their colors, the light fixtures.

Smell what is in the kitchen or what meal was last cooked.

Hear the sounds of the space and the sounds that are coming in from the outside.

Be in that room.

Look down and see the baby there. She is crying, looking for comfort, and reaching with her hands out into the air. She doesn't notice you are there. Tears are pouring out of her eyes.

What do you want to do?

Try stepping toward her. See what that feels like.

Imagine you can pick her up.

Watch what she does when she feels herself being lifted.

Take her in your arms and hold her close so she can feel your body and your breathing.

Talk to her. Tell her you're there, that she is not alone, and that you are so sorry she has been hurt.

If you are having trouble feeling for this baby, notice what you do feel. That's important too. It is possible that you are feeling some form of reluctance. Maybe the baby you sense is not crying at all and feeling very well. Maybe you need to be the baby that is being picked up. If that is the case, it might be helpful to go back and identify your resources and protectors again so you have the strength to reassure the protectors and pick up the baby. In the next step, you also learn how to be the baby as well as the caring, supportive mother or father.

Remember that any response you have to this section is the right response. Becoming curious about your authentic response will be the best way to eventually arrive at compassion for being the baby.

Step Six: Access

An imprint, like any object that sits inside a dynamic environment, requires a terrific energy to respond to or to maintain its presence in that environment. A simple example is a bowl full of apples resting on a tablecloth. When the bowl is not there, you can pull the tablecloth toward you as though it were weightless. When the bowl of apples is placed back on the table and you pull the edge of the tablecloth toward you, the drag on the tablecloth increases. You may not even be able to move it. Furthermore, if you shut your eyes, you can feel by pulling the edge of the tablecloth the approximate location of the bowl.

Most postural habits are the result of this phenomenon. When an overwhelming message is absorbed and walled off by the body, it becomes an imprint. Like a bowl of apples lying on your body's tissues, it creates a drag. If the overwhelming message continues to be walled off for weeks or months, more and more of the body's energy needs to be recruited to keep it there, out of sight and out of mind.

Remember the earlier story about the rock in the river? At first the rock is indistinguishable from the river bed. But after months of silt and debris collect around it, the location of the rock becomes more visible. A mound forms. After years, the rock will have drawn enough debris that it may create a visible ripple in the river's course. Many more years later, this ripple may shape the course of the river.

When you look at a person's body, you are, in effect, able to "see" his history, told to you by the rocks in his river.

Check out images of human anatomy at a local library, a bookstore, or online. See what's under your skin. Spend some time looking at where your organs are placed and where your spine is as well as relating those pictures to the corresponding places on your body. This will help you form a deeper relationship with your body and feel its subtler qualities.

Get touched. Touch. Trace the full length of one of your muscles. Point out the area of one of your organs. Feel under your skin what you see in the anatomy books.

Spend time in nature. Listen to the sounds that nature produces. Find a place that is free of traffic noise, and try to spend at least an hour a day there, alone or with another, sensing and feeling.

The Practice

Do you know of a reason that would make it unsafe or not a good idea to sense your body?

If the answer is yes, consider taking a break from reading. Perhaps take this opportunity to understand why you feel unsafe, what circumstances have produced this feeling, and initiate a plan to make things safe for yourself. This may take time and lots of support from people you trust.

Here are some suggestions:

- Meditation helps quiet the mind and lets you sink into a body-centered place.
- Exercise is excellent for the same reasons.
- Yoga is one of the best forms of exercise for connecting with your body.
- Go for a walk, smell flowers, eat beautifully prepared food, or be in water.
- You may consider choosing a health care practitioner who "feels right" to you, can care for your whole person, and really listens to you. Word of mouth can be a good way to locate that type of person. No two people heal the same way, so find out if he or she wants to meet you in your unique place.

If your answer is no, you can't think of a reason not to sense your body, then this next exercise is one method for accessing your body. Like all the other exercises, feel free to recreate it by changing or adding words to suit you.

Lie or sit quietly.

Enter into a state of curiosity about the sensations in your body and in your emotions.

Slowly scan your whole body, sensing and feeling.

Sensations may come in the form of pain, movement, tightening, or sleepiness.

Continue to remain curious, asking for more to be revealed. Know your body is wise and that behind every symptom is a message you will benefit from hearing.

Reserve thinking for later. Feel.

Restate your intention. Acknowledge your resources. Thank your protectors. Do this a few times.

At this moment, there is no judgment, no a priori assumptions.

Notice how your protectors (unwanted sensations or distracting habits) regularly and dutifully come to your assistance. If tension and pressure build, it is possible you are on the right track. Protectors may say, "Oh, you really need to be distracted because I don't want you to get hurt again. Here is some pain, and here is some worry. Focus on this instead of what is coming next."

Add a little more softness and a little more curiosity.

If the sensation becomes too strong, it's compassionate to stop. There is no benefit to getting overwhelmed.

Let the caring mother or father in you step in and say, "There is no need for more hurt. Hurt is what happened to me the first time."

You may also find that you are able to tolerate more sensation without feeling overwhelmed. Experiment with paying attention to your sensations without trying to find meaning in them. Just feel and be curious.

You may find nothing happens for a long time.

You may reach a threshold again and again in your attention span or in your sensations.

You may feel nothing.

Nothing is still a something. Even in the nothingness, something is happening. Your protectors may be trying to convince you not to go closer to the imprint of your earliest experiences.

Keep thanking them for doing such a good job all these years.

Allow the sensations to build while you access your resources. If sensations get unbearable, thank those protectors for doing their job. Let all the sensations be in your body at once. Now bring your resources right up alongside them, evoke them, and introduce your sensations to your resources. Hold them together. There is nothing else you need to do.

The first time you do this, it takes a leap of faith. You have no idea what awaits you on the other side. It never seems like a good idea to let your most uncomfortable sensations amplify for further inquiry, and as noted, your protectors will want you to do something else instead of feeling the effects of your earliest experiences. Your protectors may attempt to thwart your discovery by giving you unbearable pain or fear. Or they may give you other things to think about and get busy doing. Keep thanking them for attempting to protect you while you remind them that you're OK now and would like access to your imprint.

Once you become more practiced at letting yourself feel, it's possible you will consistently experience a feeling that is close to, or exactly the same as, "This feeling is too much" or "I think I'm going to die."

After you let yourself experience the full feeling of sensation in your body several times, you will grow confident that you will survive this feeling of "too much" or "I'm going to die." You will get better at thanking your protectors for doing a good job of keeping possible unwanted feelings away from your attention.

There will come a time when you have practiced enough and feel safe enough that your body senses it doesn't need to keep the sensations away from you anymore. It will begin to lure your attention through physical and emotional challenges so you are compelled to come in for a closer look.

After going through the IRP hundreds of times, you will have the luxury of trusting that on the other side is not death but freedom. When you release yourself and your protectors from shielding you from sensing the feelings of an old hurt, all the energy that was recruited to hold the stone in your river will be released. You will have access to far more life energy and will spend more time sensing your essential nature: joyousness and contentment.

You will have tested this process so many times that you will look to your body as your caring friend and thank it every time you are confronted with difficulty. You will know you are being led into a rich place. You may still go through fear and may sometimes wish to bury the feeling again in a protective response. After enough practice, however, you will find that you have far less tolerance for dominating your emotions and body. Your body will want you to be curious, and this will get easier the more you practice.

Once you realize that the voice of your symptoms is the voice of you as a small child or baby, you will be able to step forward as the supportive mother or father and hold yourself in the way you never had the opportunity to be held before.

Becoming the Baby

Continue sitting and notice what sensations arise.

The more you pay attention and invite sensations to arise, the more you will feel in your body.

Hold the part of your body where it feels like the sensations are coming from.

As you hold your sensations, you are holding you, the baby or child. You are holding the echo of experiences that your body has delicately and lovingly archived for you.

As you release the dominance of time, fear, and judgment of your sensations, they will begin to speak to you with their authentic voice. The voice may be felt, heard, or seen.

Stay attuned to the sensations. Invite them to become stronger and clearer.

Patience, curiosity, and compassion were likely missing ingredients way back then. Simply by lovingly sitting with your senses, you are already performing a healing act.

Babies move more slowly than adults. The more you slow yourself, the greater the likelihood that the baby you once were will be willing to share with you.

A baby's nervous system is sensitive, especially if it has been overwhelmed. Treat yourself as though you are that sensitive and sentient now. The world around you will cease to exist. Let it.

You are beginning to understand the language of your former self. Long-held secrets start unraveling in the slowness and the softness.

While you sit, do the following:

If there is pain, speak gently in your mind to the place that hurts. Remind yourself that this is how your body talks to you. Pain is the voice it is choosing to use. Your body is wise. This is a very young part of you. Turn toward your sensation with curiosity, love, and patience.

If there is an emotional sensation arising, remind yourself that this is how your body talks to you. This is the voice it's using. Your sensate voice is a very young voice. Turn toward your emotional sensation with curiosity, love, and patience.

If you have anxiety, consider that you have an emotion that is asking to be felt. Anxiety is commonly a protector from strong emotion. Remind yourself that your emotions would not be arising unless you were safe enough and ready to feel them. Thank the anxiety for protecting you. Gently declare to your body that you are ready to feel what wants to be felt. Notice what happens next.

As sensations or feelings arise, strongly apply your resources to them. Keep applying your memories of feeling whole while the discomforting sensations arise. Be patient. Be curious. Have compassion. Stay steady.

You are getting to know a part of yourself that has previously been unexplored.

You are remembering your wholeness.

Finding Yourself in the Wave

Often, as you reach this unexplored part of yourself, a wobbly and peaking moment comes. In its first moments, many people feel as if they are being carried by a powerful wave. This can be disorienting, as though you are losing control.

It may help you to remember that you are simultaneously two ages at moments like this. You are the age you were when you first absorbed an imprint, you are the adult you are today, and you are essentially the adult you wished you had been at the time of your imprint. So you are allowing yourself to be cared for at the same time as you are the one caring for yourself.

The wave is what the young you is feeling. The ocean giving rise to the wave is the huge tide of life rising to live you.

Keep talking to the little one in you. Acknowledge to him or her that you know the feelings he or she is having truly did happen. They are a memory. Remember where you are in the room while you let the wave carry you. Reassure the young one that you, the adult, are holding you, the young one, and the wave. Reassure the young one that you, the adult, are big enough and safe enough to do both.

Feel the sensations as they arise; do not censor them. They feel strong in contrast to the state your protectors have provided for you since the first moment you were overwhelmed. Because you've been protected, it's new to feel in this way.

Release

The underlying feelings that have been housed in your body are powerfully transformative. They have been locked up for a long time, and a lot of your energy has gone into sustaining their position, sometimes over many years. Releasing them is like releasing a slow kind of bomb in your body. The energy that was formerly being used to survive is now available for thriving.

Experiencing the emotions and other feelings just before release can be intimidating. Where you may have previously experienced pain or numbness, there may be something new. You have been living with these habitual patterns as old, secure friends right beside you for years. Even if you outgrew their benefits long ago, parting with them may seem a daunting prospect. Every time these protectors come forward, thank them. At some point, they will finally concede and let you take the responsibility they used to have of caring for you and protecting you. In a sense, you will have earned the right to be a steward to the little one they used to protect.

When release comes, because your resources have successfully convinced your protectors to trust and let go, everything suddenly feels much easier, lighter, less interrupted, and possibly even joyful.

The IRP was discovered by paying attention to what essential nature asks for; it was not invented by humans. It is one of many ways nature absorbs, stores, and releases overwhelming events in the human realm and even the nonhuman realm. Every living organism knows how to discharge imprints in this way. For other beasts, like worms, the process might have fewer steps or less complexity.

Grief

Alongside release you will often find grief. Grief can range from a sweet sensation that opens like a warm lake in your chest all the way to a body-wrenching, deep, sobbing recognition of a loss. It takes courage not only to feel these sensations but also to arrive at the surrender that precedes them. Sometimes there isn't a choice. When grief comes, it comes. It's grace. There is nothing to do except marvel at its all-encompassing, cleansing nature.

The challenges that exist with grief have been inherited from the dominance culture. The reasons for this were covered in Chapter 3, in the section "Historical Cultural Indicators." The dominance culture abhors grief because it slows down progress and makes people more vulnerable to attack as well as less able to make money and get things done. Any society that is struggling to survive, whether in a new and unfamiliar land (as was the case during colonial periods) or under the threat of war (throughout history), cannot pause to feel. Grief and other emotions make people vulnerable, so it's understandable that entire nations have forgotten how to grieve and that they pass this amnesia on to their children.

Today, entire industries of consumables thrive because people cannot weep for themselves. Clothing, accessories, foods, and most things money can buy are used to avoid grief. Gambling, working, cooking, socializing, and sex, when used with an intention to avoid emotion, can stave off grieving.

On the other hand, when they are aligned with essential nature, all the items on this list can be wonderful. Part of being human is celebrating beautiful clothing, color, good food, competition, love, and intimacy. Unfortunately, desires, if used as distractors, act like detour signs away from feeling your essential nature.

Similarly, some people confuse the emotions of their friends, children, or lover with their own emotions. They have lost touch with their essential nature.

In his teachings, the American-Guatemalan shamanic storyteller Martin Prechtel speaks about how mental illness is a symptom that appears when nations forget how to grieve. In *The Secrets of the Talking Jaguar,* he offers a foreign yet somehow refreshing image: "I can be driving down the street in my town and I can see a man walking and crying and I don't look at him and drive faster the other way, I stop and say 'Hey, brother! You're crying. You're grieving.' And I get out of my car and walk up to him. I don't think he's mentally ill or sick or something. I say 'Hey, you're grieving and I'm going to grieve with you and we're just going to be here and cry together now.'"[5]

Imagine if more societies thought of grief this way. How many times have you seen a woman crying in a grocery store, or perhaps teary in a café, and wanted to talk with her to acknowledge that you see her strong feeling and to offer empathy? Somewhere along the way, a voice taught you that "she'd rather be alone, don't bother her," or "don't talk to her, she's already embarrassed that she's crying, just let her be or you'll embarrass her more." How many people have heard parents saying about their newborn child, "He's such a good baby; he never cries"? What they don't realize is that "good babies" often stop crying after they've experienced the futility of no one responding. They haven't become more interdependent; they have given up their faith in support.

Depression is the result of a failure to grieve. Long-standing contraction in response to life-threatening messages can lead to depression. Your body may feel compressed. Compression can equal depression. Depression is not only mental/emotional; it can be physical. Grief releases depression.

Repressed grief sits at the root of most addictions. It is at the root of most symptoms, both physical and mental, and it usually sits behind anger or rage. Releasing grief is a powerful healing elixir and a gift when it comes.

Grieving Well and Safely

Were you trained to cry alone, when no one was there to look, pass judgment, or possibly reject you? Maybe you're too intimidated to cry alone because you fear that you will never stop. Or you might be someone who is very comfortable with grief. Most Western and Northern societies have adopted an alternative to communal grieving and have trained "trusted" people, like counselors and psychologists, who are employed for others to grieve in front of and with. These people are not always employed and neither are friends nor family, so it is possible you trust no one, including yourself, thus no grief happens at all.

Grief doesn't always mean big cries. Some people's protective strategies to avoid grief can look very much like grief. They may cry but not feel the real pain behind the tears. Continual sadness is another form of staving off grief. True grief is always involuntary and all-consuming. Sometimes there is crying, but sometimes, as already mentioned, grief is simply a feeling. The feeling may only last a moment, and the indicator of grief is that it provides profound relief, sometimes even joy, and certainly empathy. Your body feels enlivened. Sometimes grief has layers. Someone close to you may have died, and suddenly you are grieving everything else that's ever been tough for you as well as the loss of that person. There is a palpable difference between grieving and being upset at feeling lost or scared. Grief transforms to joy and compassion. Other kinds of sadness may feel retraumatizing or exhausting.

You may fear grief because the wave of feeling begins so strongly that it feels as though it will crush you or never end if it is allowed to begin. This fear is partially the result of rarely seeing others grieve well and safely. Because the dominance culture rewards not grieving and instead encourages certain forms of unruffled beauty, financial success, and emotional reserve, its members naturally avoid the ostracism grieving induces.

When you have found a place of safety and are in touch with your intentions, resources, and protectors, you can use sensing as a gateway to let the memory of challenging early experiences rise safely and slowly. This memory has always wanted to rise but was waiting for the right time. It has been trying to get your attention with body symptoms, negative life circumstances, relationship and communication breakdowns, or addictions. Your body is wise. Every one of its symptoms has roots, and grief is almost always one of them. (Grief has also been trying to get the attention of the dominance culture for centuries. Cultures have bodies too—people, land, and water—as well as symptoms—war, poverty, genocide, and pollution.)

Because the dominance culture is the default culture, the community that surrounds you may not support your grieving. In this case, it's prudent to have another human being with you while you grieve, although, until you grieve, you may not be able to identify the right people to surround yourself with. When you're ready, though, the more caring eyes and loving hearts you can surround yourself with, the deeper and more comfortable your healing will be.

As you grieve, you may be learning a step that you missed as a child: how to grieve safely in the company of a loving, compassionate caregiver, which ideally would have been your mother and father. But parents often did not receive the kind of empathy and sensitivity they needed from their own parents. The dominance culture did not allow for it, and they buried their feelings for the sake of survival. Deep, unmet needs have stayed with those children as they've aged and had children of their own. If parents look to their own children to make them feel better for anything, it is because they had deeply unmet needs as children.

As a child, you are perfectly designed to take on hurts. You are vulnerable, reliant on others to care for you and teach you how to be caring and compassionate. If this compassion and care were unavailable to you, even for innocent reasons, it's possible you didn't learn how to be compassionate to yourself. Now you are the caregiver! It is a bit tricky, letting go enough to feel grief and, at the same time, being the tender mother, father, or both, who picks you up or holds you until you feel you have finished your grieving. This process takes practice and gets easier over time.

It's never too late to heal.

Relief

The IRP helps you create a climate in which to resolve the effects of imprints in your being. Imagine the relief of removing the obstacles from the path along which you experience your essential nature. What would you be free to do?

If you have the opportunity to revisit in a kind way a stage you missed in your development, your brain, body, and emotional development will be ready to take off and grow! You may feel disoriented, or you may even be uncoordinated, moving in clumsy or unfamiliar ways. Trust that the disorientation and lack of coordination will pass as you become accustomed to your new skills.

You have discovered a place in you that never developed, and you are, for a time, in that stage of development. How miraculous that this patient place has been waiting, ready to grow, but in need of the right watering. By some miracle and some measure of hard work, the right water has come through to reach a very old place. See what happens next.

Compassion

Compassion arises when you are able to grieve and receive empathy while you do it. People do not experience compassion for others when they cannot grieve for their own hurts. The gateway to compassion is through the door of grief. You will respond compassionately to babies and children when you, as a baby, are compassionately responded to. If you were not treated with concern, patience, or trust when you were crying or hurt, you will react to babies, children, and emotional adults without concern, patience, or compassion.

Whether you use the IRP or other methods to access your essential nature, the results are the same. Returning home to your essential nature happens in little ways all the time and is also a lifelong dance. There are distinct stages based on your personality, your upbringing, your soul's desires, your karma, and your age. Recovering the unrequited moments in your early stages is one of the best ways to obtain the skills necessary to assist the next generation in their optimal development.

Summary

The IRP is based on observations of human nature. It is a simplified version of many practices from many cultures, and a spiritual practice not without discomfort. Despite that, from many people's accounts around the world, especially those in this book, it's been worthwhile.

Each of the IRP's six steps prepares you to lovingly and supportively detect, differentiate, and integrate your imprints. You detect them by articulating your recapitulations. When you answer questions about how, when, and in what way you were challenged, you are talking about your recapitulations. And depending on how the exercises and visualizations went for you during the IRP, you will have offered compassion to a young place in yourself, a place that was deeply challenged by overwhelming circumstances. Like the earthworm described in Chapter 1, like every living thing that has ever been, you have had experiences whose charges overwhelmed your ability to discharge them. Your body and its intelligence swiftly walled the charge off from your awareness so you would not become further overwhelmed.

The IRP and any other reparative steps with similar qualities create an environment in which you are likely to have physiological and emotional experiences that reveal memory and, often, grief and release. Grief is a skill but also a miracle, every time.

This transformation, for lack of a better word, is thanks to you aligning with your essential nature. This is one of the most intimate and enlivening processes you can embark on. It leads you to your greatest wishes, to your most optimal health, and to the greatest amount of intimacy with yourself and the people you love.

The IRP is creative and alive. The only instruction you really need is suggestions on how to sense your body. The rest of the process unfolds naturally once you trust your sensations and your body implicitly. After a time, you will trust that your symptoms are gifts, opportunities to improve your relationship with yourself. By opening your senses, you regain the nature of your innocence and the spirit of childhood. Sensing your body connects you to the present.

CHAPTER 6

Summary

Going back to the first question posed at the beginning of this book—"Who is this for?"—I hope it has become clear that you are a key person in sustaining our world. Sustaining not only in the sense of what fuels your choice to use or not use and how you consume water, food, and other resources, but also in the sense of how you interact with your consciousness and those of other living beings. Who you are with yourself, other people, and the natural world (seen and unseen), is the single strongest indicator of whether the world lives. Why? Because if you feel you matter, that you belong, that you are of consequence, then you cannot help but notice how equally dear and equally of consequence other life is. You will see all humans, plants, animals, and babies in their essential natures.

Although the IRP might seem to be another "new age" healing process—and is, in some ways, similar to many others—it is offered for one purpose: to cultivate compassion for and deep vision into your essential nature through your early self.

My wish for you and for all seven billion of us here on Earth is to see a world in which all people, young and old, hold an unshakeable knowledge of their intrinsic relevance in the whole of life. I know that one of the miracles of babies is that they continually show us the way to that world. In their secret language lives a code that unlocks our natural inclination to come back into relationship with all life.

How exciting is it to know that, within the span of one generation, a population of people can be unified to end poverty and create a sustainable economy and world peace? Care for the children in your midst, whether you ever meet them or not. They are wards of us all, now and forever.

Let's do right by them. And if that seems difficult today, then let's do what it takes to recover the people we once were. Let's foster what we want to see in the world. And if necessary, let's go back to the beginning, to the place where it was lost, and let's love that place in each and every person until the last drops of tears are soaked in love.

> . . . The long-lost Knowledge resurfaces after dropping to the bottom of the sea many storms ago. Science looks down and realizes that the light drawing up from beneath them is now traveling out of him and into her. Experience's body opens once again, the liquid light so tangible that even the quiet stops to listen. She reaches across to touch him and recognizes his shape. He is drawn toward her and exhales deeply, as though on behalf of the tired world herself.
>
> They don't speak or even move now; Knowledge reassembles between them. Suspended lovingly between liquid light and dark, Science and Experience remember their wholeness. The world breathes softly around them.
>
> Now there is a moment that neither begins nor ends. Joy is surpassed, and celebration is exceeded. Finally, these lovers, Science and Experience, and Knowledge that only lives through them, are reborn. They are the reckoning. Space and time, above and below, inside and outside, and the great sea herself all begin singing their song . . .

ACKNOWLEDGMENTS

In the years I spent writing this book, many friends and colleagues have come forward to "midwife" its pages. My deep appreciation goes to the Association for Pre- and Perinatal Psychology and Health (APPPAH) family for leading the field of prebirth and birth psychology forward and for giving practitioners and writers in the field a home for combined scientific inquiry and exploration of the ineffable.

I want to acknowledge Ray Castellino, my first prebirth and birth therapy teacher. His work has revolutionized my clinical work, and his integrity has set an uncommon height to the bar I strive to emulate. I am grateful to Yeshi Neumann, my friend and midwife of thirty-eight years, for her candid feedback and unwavering integrity that has inspired me as a woman and as a health practitioner supporting families. I am grateful to Richard Grossinger for encouraging this work and for asking "Who is this book for?" Thank you to Judyth Weaver for critiquing this work and for her emphasis on lineage. And to all the staff at North Atlantic Books for continuing on in integrity to publish works that serve the wholeness of society. I am grateful to Raffi Covoukinan for asking, after he read an early draft, "What is the culture you are promoting if not the dominance culture?" I am grateful to those who have read this book and encouraged me to say what needs to be said and to those whose stories about how their early experiences shaped them I have been permitted to share.

My appreciation goes to all the staff and mothers at the Lower Mainland Childbearing Society for continuing to invite me into their circles and for doing this, humanity's most powerful act: gathering as faithful storytellers of these ancient rites of passage.

NOTES

Introduction

1. As told by Jack Kornfield about the Himba people of Namibia.

Chapter 1

1. Jealous 2000.
2. In 1835, German scientist Carl Friedrich Gauss was the first to measure the magnetic field around the earth.
3. McCraty, Bradley, and Tomasino 2004–5.
4. Ibid.
5. Sheldrake 2009b.
6. Ibid.
7. Sheldrake 2009a.
8. Szyf 2008.
9. Lipton 2013.
10. Herman 1997.
11. Armstrong 2007.
12. These are by no means exclusive influences on how life is shaped. But additional influences are beyond the scope of this book.

Chapter 2

1. Ikegawa 2006a, 2006b.
2. Ibid.
3. Sheldrake 1995.
4. Evans 2008.
5. Sadler 2006.
6. Ibid.
7. Pearce 2002.
8. Bainbridge Cohen 1993.

9. Ibid.

10. Sadler 2006.

11. Evans 2008.

12. Herman 1997.

13. Sadler 2006.

14. Pearce 2002.

15. Ibid.

16. Bainbridge Cohen 1993.

17. Siegel 2007.

18. Ibid.

19. Pearce 2002.

20. Ibid.

21. Siegel 2007.

22. Bainbridge Cohen 1993.

23. Ibid.

24. Odent 1986.

25. Buckley 2003; Odent 2001b.

26. Geber 1956.

27. Schore 2002.

28. Emerson 2001.

29. Mohler 2005.

30. Schore 2002; Lipton 2002.

31. From conversations I had with A. Feldmar in 2006, discussing psychiatric systems in the UK.

32. Castellino and Takikawa 1997.

33. Odent 2001b.

34. Jackson 2004.

35. All the babies in my private practice have recapitulated one or more of these imprints in their sequencing, demonstrating the intrusive nature with which these interventions were administered after birth.

36. Firestone 1985.

37. The combined use of the terms *conception, implantation,* and *discovery* are used throughout Raymond Castellino's therapeutic and written words, and are inspired by the works of Wilhelm Reich, Randolph Stone, and Rudolph Steiner, to name a few.

38. Castellino 1995.
39. Marais 1926.
40. Ibid.
41. Lorenz 1970–71.
42. Blauvelt 1956.
43. Bridges 1977.
44. Byrnes, Elizabeth, and Bridges 2000.
45. Poindron and Le Neindre 1979; Krehbiel et al. 1987.
46. Odent 2001b.

Chapter 3

1. The term is complementary to, but not synonymous with, Riane Eisler's term "the Dominator Culture," which describes patriarchal, violent, male-deity-worshipping societies that began to invade the peaceful, creative, female-deity-worshipping societies in Neolithic Europe in several waves (4300–4200 BC, 3400–3200 BC, and 3000–2800 BC).
2. Eisler 1987.
3. Ibid.
4. Mercenaries were sent by the Roman Empire to indoctrinate and regulate tribal peoples. "Europe" did not exist; tribal areas with distinct peoples were eventually ousted, blended, and converted first to Roman culture, and later, on its dwindling vine, to Christianity.
5. Quinn 1990.
6. Papal Bulls Dum diversas 1452; Romanus Pontifex 1455; Inter Caetera 1493. See Dorsett 2007 regarding the papal bulls citations.
7. In July 2008, the International Council of the 13 Indigenous Grandmothers traveled to the Vatican and asked to meet with the pope to discuss revoking the papal bulls. They were denied meetings and demonstrated peacefully in the Vatican courtyard.
8. Tarnas 1991.
9. Some 2004; Crehan 2002; Abernethy 2002. Gramsci, 1891–1937, was an Italian writer, politician, and political theorist who elaborated the Marxist term *hegemony* (from the earlier Greek *hegeisthai,* "to lead or track down"), through which he describes how capitalism maintained control not just through violence and political and economic

coercion but, ideologically, also through a hegemonic culture in which the values of the bourgeoisie became the "common sense" values of all.

10. Takikawa 2004.

11. Castellino 2003.

12. Chamberlain 1995.

13. Castellino 2004.

14. Duer 1879; Weber 1971.

15. Odent 2007.

16. Pelosi and Ortega 1994; Pelosi and Pelosi 1995.

17. Pelosi and Pelosi 1995; Luzes 2007.

18. Gibbons et al. 2010.

19. Emerson 1998; Castellino 1995; Buckley 2003.

20. Findeisen 2004.

21. Castellino and Takikawa 1997.

22. Brody 2008.

23. Croal and Hughes1997.

24. Acolet, Sleath, and Whitelaw 1989; "Management of Asymptomatic Hypoglycemia" 2006; Montagu 1986.

25. World Health Organization 2002. Note that these figures represent people, not percentages.

26. Since the writing of this book, I have learned through colleagues that even Dutch mothers are refused home births when having twins, which indicates that midwives are not as trusted as they ideally could be.

27. Lyman 2011.

28. Statistics Canada 2002. Note that these figures represent people, not percentages.

29. National Centre for Health Statistics 2002. Note that these figures represent people, not percentages.

30. Jacobsen and Nyberg 1988.

31. Jacobsen and Nyberg 1990.

32. Nyberg et al. 1992, 1993.

33. Jacobsen et al. 1987; Jacobsen and Bygdeman 2000.

34. Nyberg, Buka, and Lipsitt 2000.

35. Raine et al. 1994.

36. Kalef 2008.
37. De Mause 1996.
38. Ibid.
39. Ibid.
40. De Mause 2002.
41. De Mause 1996.
42. Ibid.

Chapter 4

1. Ruiz 1997.
2. Lovelock 2006.
3. Abram 1997.
4. Lewis and Lewis 1996.

Chapter 5

1. Leviticus, *The Tanakh*.
2. Kamiya 2005.
3. Matarasso 1995.
4. Stephen Jenkinson imparted this knowledge during a talk given at his Orphan Wisdom School in Golden Lake, Ontario, October 6, 2012.
5. Prechtel 1998.

REFERENCES

Abernethy, D. B. 2002. *The Dynamics of Global Dominance: European Overseas Empires, 1415–1980.* New Haven, CT: Yale University Press.

Abram, D. 1997. *The Spell of the Sensuous.* New York: Vintage.

Acolet, D., K. Sleath, and A. Whitelaw. 1989. "Oxygenation, Heart Rate, and Temperature in Very Low Birth Weight Infants during Skin-to-Skin Contact with Their Mothers." *Acta Paediatrica Scandinavica* 78:189–93.

Armstrong, Jeffrey. 2007. *Karma: The Ancient Science of Cause and Effect.* San Rafael, CA: Mandala Publishing.

Bainbridge Cohen, Bonnie. 1993. *Sensing, Feeling and Action: The Experiential Anatomy of Body-Mind Centering.* North Hampton, MA: Contact Editions.

Blauvelt, H. 1956. "Neonate-Mother Relationship in Goat and Man." In *Group Processes,* edited by B. Shaffner. New York: Josiah Macy Jr. Foundation.

Bridges, R. S. 1977. "Parturition: Its Role in the Long-Term Retention of Maternal Behaviour in the Rat." *Physiology and Behavior* 18:147–49.

Brody, L. J. 2008. "365 Days From Now." Lecture given to the Electro Federation of Canada. Victoria, BC.

Buckley, S. J. 2003. "Undisturbed Birth: Nature's Blueprint for Ease and Ecstasy." *Journal of Prenatal and Perinatal Psychology and Health* 17 (4): 261–88.

Byrnes, E., M. Elizabeth, and R. S. Bridges. 2000. "Endogenous Opioid Facilitation of Maternal Memory in Rats." *Behavioural Neuroscience* 114 (4): 797–804.

Castellino, R. 1995. *The Polarity Therapy Paradigm Regarding Preconception, Prenatal and Birth Imprinting.* Santa Barbara, CA: Castellino Prenatal and Birth Therapy Training.

———. 2003. Lecture during Process Workshop. Santa Barbara, CA. July.

———. 2004. Lecture during Process Workshop. Santa Barbara, CA. April.

Castellino, R., and D. Takikawa. 1997. *The Caregiver's Role in Birth and Newborn Self-Attachment Needs.* Santa Barbara, CA: Building and Enhancing Bonding and Attachment.

Chamberlain, D. 1995. "What Babies Are Teaching Us about Violence." *Journal of Prenatal and Perinatal Psychology and Health* 10 (2): 57–74.

Crehan, Kate. 2002. *Gramsci, Culture, and Anthropology.* Berkeley: University of California Press.

Croal, N'Gai, and Jane Hughes. 1997. "Lara Croft, the Bit Girl: How a Game Star Became a '90s Icon." *Newsweek.* November 10.

De Mause, L. 1996. "Restaging Fetal Traumas in War and Social Violence." *Journal of Prenatal and Perinatal Psychology and Health* 10 (4): 229–59.

———. 2002. *The Emotional Life of Nations.* New York: Other Press.

Dorsett, Shaunnagh. 2007. "Mapping Territories." In *Jurisprudence of Jurisdiction,* edited by Shaun McVeigh, 144. New York: Routledge.

Duer, E. L. 1879. "Postmortem Delivery." *American Journal of Obstetrics and Gynecology* 12 (1): 1–22.

Eckman, P. 2007. "Compassion in Education." Lecture summarizing conversations with HH The Dalai Lama. Wosk Centre for Dialogue, Vancouver, BC.

Eisler, R. 1987. *The Chalice and the Blade.* San Francisco: Harper San Francisco.

———. 2007. *Real Wealth of Nations.* San Francisco: Berrett-Koehler Publishers.

Emerson, W. R. 1998. "Birth Trauma: The Psychological Effects of Obstetrical Interventions." *Journal of Prenatal and Perinatal Psychology and Health* 13 (1): 11–43.

———. 2001. "Treating Cesarean Birth Trauma during Infancy and Childhood." *Journal of Prenatal and Perinatal Psychology and Health* 15 (3): 177–94.

Evans, J. 2008. Keynote address to regional APPPAH Congress. Nelson, BC.

Findeisen, B. 2004. Interview in Takikawa 2004.

Firestone, R. 1985. *The Fantasy Bond.* Los Angeles: Glendon Association.

Geber, M. 1956. "Research in Uganda Using the Gesell Developmental Scale." *Journal of Social Psychology:* 180–93.

Gibbons, Luz, José M. Belizán, Jeremy A. Lauer, Ana P. Betrán, Mario Merialdi, and Fernando Althabe. 2010. "The Global Numbers and Costs of

Additionally Needed and Unnecessary Caesarean Sections Performed per Year: Overuse as a Barrier to Universal Coverage." *World Health Report, Background Paper 30.* WHO. http://www.who.int/healthsystems/topics /financing/healthreport/30C-sectioncosts.pdf.

Grossinger, Richard. 2000. *Embryogenesis: Species, Gender, and Identity.* Berkeley, CA: North Atlantic Books.

———. 2003. *Embryos, Galaxies, and Sentient Beings: How the Universe Makes Life.* Berkeley, CA: North Atlantic Books.

Herman, Judith. 1997. *Trauma and Recovery: The Aftermath of Violence from Domestic Abuse to Political Terror.* New York: Basic Books.

Ikegawa, Akira. 2006a. *I Chose You to Be My Mommy.* Japan: Lyon Company Ltd.

———. 2006b. *Parenting Begins from a Baby's Time in the Womb: What We Know from Prenatal Memories.* Tokyo, Japan: Sunmark Publishing.

Jackson, M. 2004. Interview in Takikawa 2004.

Jacobsen, B., and M. Bygdeman. 2000. "Obstetric Care and Proneness of Offspring to Suicide as Adults: A Case Control Study." *Journal of Prenatal and Perinatal Psychology and Health* 15 (1): 63–74.

Jacobsen, B., G. Eklund, L. Hamberger, D. Linnarsson, G. Sedvall, and M. Valverius M. 1987. "Perinatal Origin of Adult Self-Destructive Behavior." *Acta Psychiatrica Scandinavica* 76 (4): 364–71.

Jacobsen, B., and K. Nyberg. 1988. "Obstetrical Pain Medication and Eventual Adult Amphetamine Addiction in Offspring." *Acta Obstetricia et Gynecologica Scandinavica* 67 (8): 677–82.

———. 1990. "Opiate Addiction in Adult Offspring through Possible Imprinting after Obstetric Treatment." *BMJ* 301 (6760): 1067–70.

Jealous, J. 2000. "Every Drop 'Knows the Tide.'" *The Biodynamics of Osteopathy.* Lecture series. Marnee Jealous Long / Longtide Management 608729242307, MP3. http://jamesjealous.com/lecture-series-by-dr-jealous.

Kalef, M. 2008. "The Family Field." Lecture given at the APPPAH Regional Congress. Nelson, BC.

Kamiya, T. 2005. *Indian Architecture.* Hyderabad, India: Pragati.

Kornfield, Jack. 1993. *A Path with Heart.* New York: Bantam Books.

Krehbiel, D., P. Poindron, F. Levy, and M. J. Prud'homme. 1987. "Peridural Anesthesia Disturbs Maternal Behaviour in Primiparous and Multiparous Parturient Ewes." *Physiology and Behavior* 40:463–72.

Leviticus 16:13–16. *The Tanakh.*

Lewis, C., and C. A. Lewis. 1996. *Green Nature/Human Nature: The Meaning of Plants in Our Lives.* Chicago: University of Illinois Press.

Lipton, B. 2002. *Nature, Nurture and the Power of Love: The Biology of Conscious Parenting.* Memphis, TN: Spirit 2000, Inc. DVD.

———. 2013. *The Biology of Belief.* Carlsbad, CA: Hay House.

Lorenz, K. 1970–71. *Studies in Animal and Human Behaviour.* Cambridge: Cambridge University Press.

Lovelock, James. 2006. *The Revenge of Gaia: Earth's Climate Crisis and the Fate of Humanity.* New York: Basic Books.

Luzes, E. 2007. Lecture given at the APPPAH World Congress. Los Angeles, CA.

Lyman, B. J. 2008. "Prenatal and Perinatal Trauma Case Formulation: Toward an Evidenced-Based Assessment of the Origins of Repetitive Behaviours in Adults." *Journal of Prenatal and Perinatal Psychology and Health* 25 (4): 235–63.

"Management of Asymptomatic Hypoglycemia in Healthy Term Neonates for Nurses and Midwives." 2006. *Australian Nursing Journal* 13 (2): 13.

Marais, E. 1926. "The Soul of the White Ant." First published in *Transvaal Newspaper.* http://journeytoforever.org/farm_library/Marais1/whiteant-ToC.html.

Matarasso, F. 1995. *The English Castle.* London: Cassell.

McCraty, Rollin, Raymond T. Bradley, and Dana Tomasino. 2004–05. "The Resonant Heart." *Shift* (December–February): 15–19. http://www.heartmath.org/templates/ihm/downloads/pdf/research/publications/the-resonant-heart.pdf.

Mohler, E. 2005. *Essentials of Vascular Laboratory Diagnosis.* Oxford: Blackwell Publishing.

Montagu, A. 1986. *Touching: The Human Significance of the Skin.* New York: Harper and Row.

National Centre for Health Statistics. 2002. *Deaths: Injuries, 2002.* http://www.cdc.gov/nchs/deaths.htm#News%20Releases.

Nyberg, K., P. Allebeck, G. Eklund, and B. Jacobsen. 1992. "Socio-Economic versus Obstetric Risk Factors for Drug Addiction in Offspring." *British Journal of Addiction* 87 (12): 1669–76.

———. 1993. "Obstetric Medication versus Residential Area as Perinatal Risk Factors for Subsequent Adult Drug Addiction in Offspring." *Paediatric Perinatal Epidemiology* 7 (1): 23–32.

Nyberg, K., S. L. Buka, and L. P. Lipsitt. 2000. "Perinatal Medication as a Potential Risk Factor for Adult Drug Abuse in a North American Cohort." *Epidemiology* 11 (6): 715–16.

Odent, M. 1986. *Primal Health.* London: Century Hutchison.

———. 2001a. "New Reasons and New Ways to Study Birth Physiology." *International Journal of Gynecology and Obstetrics* 75 (S1): 39–45.

———. 2001b. *The Scientification of Love.* London: Free Association Books.

———. 2007. Lecture given at the APPPAH World Congress. Los Angeles, CA.

Olsen, Andrea. 1991. *Bodystories: A Guide to Experiential Anatomy.* Barrytown, NY: Station Hill Press.

Pearce, Joseph Chilton. 2002. *The Biology of Transcendence: A Blueprint of the Human Spirit.* Rochester, VT: Park Street Press.

Pelosi, M. A., and I. Ortega. 1994. "Cesarean Section: Pelosi Simplified Technique." *Revista chilena de obstetricia y ginecología* 59:372–77.

Pelosi, M. A., II, and M. A. Pelosi III. 1995. "Simplified Cesarean Section." *Contemporary OB/GYN* 40:89–100.

Poindron, P., and P. Le Neindre. 1979. "Hormonal and Behavioural Basis for Establishing Maternal Behaviour in Sheep." In *Psychoneuroendocrinology in Reproduction,* edited by L. Zichella and R. Panchari. Amsterdam, Netherlands: Elsevier-North Holland Medical Press.

Prechtel, M. 1998. *The Secrets of the Talking Jaguar.* London: Thorsons.

Quinn, D. 1990. *Explorers and Colonies: America, 1500–1625.* New York: Continuum International Publishing Group.

Raine, A., P. Brennan, and S. A. Mednick. 1994. "Birth Complications Combined with Early Maternal Rejection at Age 1 Year Predisposes to Violent Crime at Age 18 Years." *Archives of General Psychiatry* 51 (12): 984–88.

Ruiz, Miguel. 1997. *Beyond Fear: A Toltec Guide to Freedom and Joy.* Tulsa, OK: Council Oak Books.

Sadler, T. W. 2006. *Langman's Medical Embryology.* 10th ed. Philadelphia: Lippincott Williams and Wilkins.

Schore, A. N. 2002. "The Neurobiology of Attachment and Early Personality Organization." *Journal of Prenatal and Perinatal Psychology and Health* 16 (3): 249–59.

Sheldrake, Rupert. 1995. *A New Science of Life: The Hypothesis of Morphic Resonance.* Rochester, VT: Park Street Press.

———. 2009a. "Morphic Resonance." Workshop presented at Hollyhock Retreat Center. Cortes Island, BC.

———. 2009b. *Morphic Resonance: The Nature of Formative Causation.* Toronto: Park Street Press.

Siegel, D. 2007. *The Mindful Brain: Reflection and Attunement in the Cultivation of Well-Being.* New York: W. W. Norton.

Some, S. 2004. Interview in Takikawa 2004.

Statistics Canada. 2002. *Suicides and Suicide Rate, by Sex and by Age Group.* http://www40.statcan.ca/l01/cst01/perhlth66c.htm.

Szyf, Moshe. 2008. Lecture given at Science Meets Our Hearts APPPAH Congress. Nelson, BC.

Takikawa, D. 2004. *What Babies Want: An Exploration of the Consciousness of Infants.* Video. Available from Los Olivos, CA: Hana Peace Works. http://www.whatbabieswant.com.

Tarnas, Richard. 1991. *The Passion of the Western Mind: Understanding the Ideas That Have Shaped Our World View.* New York: Ballantine.

Weber, C. E. 1971. "Postmortem Cesarean Section: Review of the Literature and Case Reports." *American Journal of Obstetrical Gynecology* 110 (2): 158–65.

World Health Organization. 2002. *World Report on Violence and Health.* Geneva: WHO. http://www.who.int.

Suggested Reading

Anthony, David W. 2007. *The Horse, the Wheel, and Language: How Bronze Age Riders from the Eurasian Steppes Shaped the Modern World.* Princeton, NJ: Princeton University Press.

Augustoni, Daniel. 2013. *Craniosacral Therapy for Children: Treatments for Expecting Mothers, Babies, and Children.* Berkeley, CA: North Atlantic Books.

Becker, Robert O., and Gary Selden. 1985. *The Body Electric: Electromagnetism and the Foundation of Life.* New York: Quill Press.

Brennan, Barbara Ann. 1987. *Hands of Light: A Guide to Healing through the Human Energy Field.* Toronto: Bantam Books.

———. 1993. *Light Emerging: The Journey of Personal Healing.* New York: Bantam Books.

Cassidy, Tina. 2006. *Birth: The Surprising History of How We Are Born.* New York: Atlantic Monthly Press.

Dossey, Larry. 1982. *Space, Time, and Medicine.* Boston: Shambhala Press.

Grille, Robin. 2005. *Parenting for a Peaceful World.* New South Wales, Australia: Longueville Media.

Hanna, Thomas. 1988. *Somatics: Reawakening the Mind's Control of Movement, Flexibility, and Health.* New York: Addison-Wesley.

Janov, Arthur. 2011. *Life before Birth: The Hidden Script That Rules Our Lives.* Chicago: NTI Upstream.

Janus, Ludwig. 2001. *The Enduring Effects of Prenatal Experience: Echoes from the Womb.* Heidelberg: Verlage Mattes Press.

Jealous, James. 2008. "Wholeness No. 1." *The Biodynamics of Osteopathy in the Cranial Field: An Interactive Audio Text by James Jealous D.O.* Lecture series. Marnee Jealous Long / Longtide Management 608729242307, MP3. http://jamesjealous.com/lecture-series-by-dr-jealous.

Lowen, Alexander. 1995. *Joy: The Surrender to the Body and to Life.* New York: The Penguin Group.

Milne, Hugh. 1995. *The Heart of Listening: A Visionary Approach to Craniosacral Work.* Berkeley, CA: North Atlantic Books.

Mitchell, Barry, and Ram Sharma. 2005. *Embryology: An Illustrated Colour Text.* Edinburgh, Scotland: Elsevier Churchill Livingstone.

Odent, M. 2002. *Primal Health: Understanding the Critical Period between Conception and the First Birthday.* East Sussex, UK: Clairview Books.

Peirsman, Etienne, and Neeto Peirsman. 2005. *Craniosacral Therapy for Babies and Small Children.* Berkeley, CA: North Atlantic Books.

Schultz, R. Louis, and Rosemary Feitis. 1996. *The Endless Web: Fascial Anatomy and Physical Reality.* Berkeley, CA: North Atlantic Books.

Sills, Franklin. 2002. *The Polarity Process: Energy as a Healing Art.* Berkeley, CA: North Atlantic Books.

Siu, R. G. H. 1957. *The Tao of Science.* Cambridge: Massachusetts Institute of Technology Press.

Some, Malidoma Patrice. 1994. *Of Water and the Spirit: Ritual, Magic and Initiation in the Life of an African Shaman.* New York: Penguin Press.

Upledger, John E. 1997. *Your Inner Physician and You.* Berkeley, CA: North Atlantic Books.

———. 2007. *SomatoEmotional Release: Deciphering the Language of Life.* Berkeley, CA: North Atlantic Books.

INDEX

ABOUT THE AUTHOR

Photo by Michael Julian Berz

Mia Kalef practiced as a chiropractor and craniosacral therapist for eighteen years. During that time she founded Emerging Families, a center for therapy, research, and education for the primal period. She now mentors health practitioners in bringing prebirth and birth awareness into their work. Kalef's course, The Intuitive Recovery Project, offers modules for opening the senses to relational intimacy with nature, self, and others. Additionally, her four-week online recovery program for families after challenging births is found at www.secretlifeofbabies.com. She lives in Vancouver with her partner, Bruce, where she is a student of incarnation, beauty, emergence, and indigenousity.

North Atlantic Books
Berkeley, California

Personal, spiritual, and planetary transformation

North Atlantic Books, a nonprofit publisher established in 1974, is dedicated to fostering community, education, and constructive dialogue. NABCommunities.com is a meeting place for an ever-growing membership of readers and authors to engage in the discussion of books and topics from North Atlantic's core publishing categories.

NAB Communities offer interactive social networks in these genres:

NOURISH: Raw Foods, Healthy Eating and Nutrition, All-Natural Recipes

WELLNESS: Holistic Health, Bodywork, Healing Therapies

WISDOM: New Consciousness, Spirituality, Self-Improvement

CULTURE: Literary Arts, Social Sciences, Lifestyle

BLUE SNAKE: Martial Arts History, Fighting Philosophy, Technique

Your free membership gives you access to:

Advance notice about new titles and exclusive giveaways

Podcasts, webinars, and events

Discussion forums

Polls, quizzes, and more!

Go to www.NABCommunities.com and join today.